# BEHIND A THIN GREEN LINE

*A Memoir of an Undercover Game Warden*

By

## TONY H. LATHAM

iv

Cover Design by Jay Griffith

# Dedication

This book is dedicated to Conley Elms and Bill Pogue, two Idaho game wardens gunned downed by a poacher while protecting wildlife.

# *Foreword*

This book is about a collision of poachers and game wardens. The glue that binds this tale is elk. The reader may find it of value to know the history of these marvelous animals, and how close we came to losing them.

In the great scheme of Earth, elk have been in North America for the blink of an afternoon. Fossil records indicate that roughly 15,000 years ago, woolly mammoths and elk expanded their range from northeast Siberia into North America. And sometime after that–after the eyed needle had been invented and used to stitch together warm clothing–humans began to populate North America from the eastern edge of Siberia.

For thousands of years, people in the Americas didn't have bows and arrows; they hunted with an atlatl. These forearm-long tools were made of wood or bone and greatly increased the speed of a hand-thrown spear. They work much like modern plastic tennis-ball throwers that are made for playing with a dog. The three-foot to four-foot long spears that atlatls throw are called darts. At the aft end of an atlatl, a spur sticks up that fits into a hole in the back of the dart's shaft. This shaft is about four feet long, stabilized with feathers like an arrow and tipped with a double-edged stone point. A good atlatl hunter can put a heavy dart into an animal's chest at 40 paces. Undoubtedly, the first elk felled by man was done with a long dart thrown with an atlatl.

The earliest indisputable evidence of man in Alaska are stone tools and fire hearths that carbon date 8,000-11,000 years B.P (before present). In two of these sites, archeologists found elk bones associated with tools. In Wyoming, elk bones and antler pieces have been recovered from sites dating to about 10,800 years B.P.

Debatably, the first culture that developed in North America is called Clovis and these people were primarily–but not entirely–mammoth hunters. The Folsom culture came next and is believed to have developed from the Clovis after the continent's elephants were extinct. Folsom hunters were primarily buffalo hunters and used deeply fluted stone points on their atlatl darts. These points were so difficult to make that it's believed they must have had an unknown significance beyond their lethality. Clovis and Folsom peoples hunted elk, but only on an incidental basis. Subsequent indigenous peoples continued to utilize elk, but very few relied on them as their primary food source.

Ernest Thompson Seton estimated that when Europeans stumbled upon North America, there were about 10 million elk. Evidence shows they were distributed across the continent and were common from the Pacific coast, throughout the Great Plains and the forests of the east coast. With all these elk, why didn't people focus on these big animals as a primary food source?

I've hunted elk for forty-five years using rifles and bows. Except for a few lean years, my freezer had elk in it. If I had been forced to use an atlatl, I'm certain my icebox would have been empty. Here's my theory: people with atlatls could make a living hunting elephants and buffalo since they tend to take a stand-their-ground defense similar to muskoxen forming a circle. But elk don't do that. They blitz. I think that hunter using an atlatl could starve to death before he consistently closed within thirty or forty paces of these long-legged critters.

In the mid-19th century, the situation changed and elk began walking towards a graveyard. The equation that triggered this perfect storm had two veins. The first was what transplanted Europeans called "the Indian problem." In short, Native Americans were obstructing the perceived divine providence we called Manifest Destiny. At the same time, the manufacture of goods had shifted from crafting products by hand in small shops to mass production in factories powered by steam engines and water wheels. The Industrial Revolution was off and rolling. The one material lacking was thick leather for the belting that was needed to distribute power to the machinery.

Buffalo became the solution to both problems and the race to weed the plains began. Twenty thousand men, mostly veterans running from the death and guts of the Civil War, began their bloody work with Sharps rifles and skinning knives.

During this wholesale slaughter, a buffalo skin went for $3.50, while a skin ripped from an elk was worth $7–all in a period where the average annual income was $170 a year. If an elk stepped within range of a hide hunter's rifle, a dark cloud of smoke burst from its muzzle, its skin was thrown on the pile and the carcass left for the wolves.

In 1873, Columbus Delano, President Grant's Secretary of Interior wrote,

*"The civilization of the Indian is impossible
while the buffalo remain upon the plains. I
would not seriously regret the total
disappearance of the buffalo from our
western prairies, in its effect upon the
Indians, regarding it as a means of
hastening their sense of dependence upon
the products of the soil and their own
labors."*

Steven Rinella wrote in his iconic book, *American Buffalo*,

*"Along the South Fork of the Platte River,
hundreds of hide hunters lined fifty miles
of riverbank and used fires to keep the
buffalo from getting water at night. In
four daytime periods, they gunned down
fifty thousand of the thirst-crazed
animals."*

Luther Standing Bear saw it first hand and wrote about it in his autobiography, *My People the Sioux.*

*"Our scouts, who had gone out to locate the
buffalo, came back and reported that the
plains were covered with dead bison. We
kept moving, fully expecting soon to run
across plenty of live buffalo; but were
disappointed. I saw the bodies of hundred
of dead buffalo lying about, just wasting,
and the odor was terrible."*

It is estimated that between 30 and 60 million buffalo were killed in twenty-five years. How many other animals were sucked into this holocaust is unknown, but by 1890, Grant and Delano had their wish. Buffalo, elk and grizzlies were gone from the Great Plains and the only thing left were sun-bleached bones and Indians decimated by disease and hunger.

During this same period, gold was discovered in Idaho, Montana, and Wyoming. Thousands of people rushed to the promise of wealth.

This influx needed meat. The demand rapidly outstripped what the ranchers could supply and the only additional source of protein was wild game. Anyone with a rifle and a pack animal could make a quick dollar. Around boomtowns with names like Gibbonsville, Leesburg, and Bayhorse, market hunting became more profitable for some than shoveling pay dirt into a sluice.

Elk were headed into a box canyon and the people of Idaho weren't blind. The situation became so grim that when Idaho's first territorial legislature met in 1863, one of their initial efforts was to pass The Game Act, which established big game seasons and made the sale of game meat illegal when the seasons were closed. The penalty for non-compliance was a civil forfeiture from $5 to $200. What was glaringly absent in this law—in hindsight—was somebody to enforce it.

Wildlife numbers continued to circle the drain. At the end of the 19th century, elk were nearly extinct in Idaho. In an effort to curtail this, the Idaho legislature passed a law in 1899 shortening the elk season from seven months to one month. It also recognized what market hunting had done and made it illegal to sell game meat. In the same legislation, they created a State Game Warden position with an annual salary of $1200 and directed him to hire a deputy warden for each of the counties,

> "Such special deputy shall receive as his
> compensation one-half of all fines
> recovered upon prosecution procured by
> him for violation of the fish and game
> laws of this state and shall receive no
> other compensation."

In picturing this era, an Idaho game warden got a paycheck only when he made a case. Since elk were as scarce as frog's teeth, it must have made for a slim serving of beans while riding a bony horse.

In 1918, the Idaho legislature closed elk seasons in all but four of the forty-four counties. They also set the pay for game wardens to $3 per day. That same year, the U.S. Forest Service conducted the first statewide elk census and estimated 618 animals. It seems highly likely that for political reasons, the legislature ignored this biological data and had open elk seasons in counties that didn't have elk.

What is also clear as glass is that the people of Idaho were revolting over politicians managing wildlife. By 1912, there were over 10,000 members of the Idaho Sportsmen's Association, and their heart-felt mission was to get the legislators out of game management. The previous year, Game Warden Frank Kendall recommended to the governor that

> "Placing the fish and game department of
> Idaho on a scientific basis and in order to
> do so we must have men who have made

*this a study and are familiar with the
needs and requirement of this line of
work, regardless of political affiliations,
and to this end I would recommend we
place the men who are directly in the fish
and game department under a civil
service ruling and retain them as long as
they do good work."*

Two years later, Game Warden J.B Gowen was fed up
with political meddling and told the governor,

*"When we get men who are competent, who
understand the business, they should be
retained regardless of politics."*

The one place in the nation that had been shielded from
the decimation of elk was Yellowstone National Park. The
first superintendent reported in 1877 that there were
"thousands of elk." In 1900, Superintendent O.J. Brown
estimated there were between 35,000 and 60,000 elk in the
park.

With the growth of wildlife agencies and a clamoring
from sportsman's groups, Yellowstone Park started a
program of trapping elk for the purpose of reintroduction
to their native ranges. In 1915, the park shipped 50 elk by
rail to Idaho. Within four years, the state had received 200
elk. The transplants continued through 1946 with a total of
733 Yellowstone elk that were released into historic habitat.

By 1975, the Idaho Department of Fish and Game
estimated there were over 50,000 elk in the state. This
population growth was the result of the Yellowstone
translocation program and the efforts of biologists and

game wardens—all spurred by the people of Idaho who had a passion for elk. Today, there are over 100,000 elk in the state.

# *Preface*

This story is true. However, the names of the defendants have been changed for my protection. The tale in these pages is about *elk poachers*, their methods and attitudes–not *elk hunters*, so please don't get the two confused.

The conversations on these pages were well documented in reports and transcriptions. The poacher's voices can be confusing. That's the way it was.

# *Prologue*

It was as cold and heavy as a river rock and had been waiting for me in a snow-covered truck. I hadn't seen it for nearly a decade, but it caused me stop. It was a large three-ring binder as thick as a prizefighter's fist with the words *Report of Investigation* printed in a large bold font. Below the title were eight names.

After a moment, I opened the cover and it was as if I'd stepped into a time machine. The first document was my thirty-eight page report followed by several shorter reports written by other officers. Past the report section, there were eight colored plastic tabs that jutted off to the side, each with a defendant's name.

The first tab had his name on it, and I couldn't get past it. He was an unwelcome memory.

I flipped the tab and his pale eyes drilled back from a page-sized driver's license photo.

When I had run with him, he wore a dirty yellow ball cap. In this photo, it was obvious he'd just taken it off. His hair was matted across his forehead and covered most of his ears in an unkempt Beatles look but there wasn't anything carefree about the expression he wore. His green eyes were set deep in his skull and surrounded by wrinkles that had been etched from the bottom of a bottle of his own remarkable hell. He hadn't shaved for at least a week, and gray was beginning to invade his chin. There was no smile on his face. It looked like he'd spent the night on the floor of a singlewide trailer and needed a drink.

Those eyes had stared at me when I slipped into the cab of his beat-up truck. He sat behind the steering wheel with his left leg pushing his rifle into the door. The butt was on the floor, and the barrel was pointing up.

His grin lied about his mood; his eyes were frowning and had a piercing ugliness. Something was wrong.

He took a sip from his guzzler, and slurred, "let's go find those fuckers."

# Chapter 1

Cases come in different ways. This one started with a phone call from a game warden by the name of Merritt Horsmon.

"Checked a camp in the Pahsimeroi this afternoon."

I got out of my pickup, stepped back to the bed and reached up to my dog's chin. "You spank 'em, Merritt?"

"No, that's the problem. I got a call from a rancher. Says he watched them chase elk, shootin' while hauling ass and trespassing." He paused and I heard a room door close. "I checked their camp. Felt like I was in Appalachia."

As he spoke, I thought about this high-desert valley framed by two parallel mountain ranges that people collectively referred to as *the Pahsimeroi*. Even as a kid growing up in Idaho Falls, the name had rolled like a hoop down a hill.

But as my mind drifted off to the remote valley, Horsmon's voice brought me back. He hadn't laughed when he'd referred to the camp as Appalachia. This wasn't the same young warden I knew. His speech was hushed and deep. It had a slight growl to it. It was obvious that he hadn't called to BS with me or spin an amusing game warden story. He was grouchy.

"No citations?" I asked.

Horsmon's pitch got deeper, "I don't think you're listening. The landowner watched this shit from over a mile away. He could see the dust from the elk. Said there were three rigs chasing, and they fired a dozen shots or so—most while they were still hauling ass. Said it looked like a stampede and sounded like a war. By the time he got there, they were gone, but somehow he knew who they were and where they're camped."

"They hit anything?"

"He thought they'd knocked one down. I found some blood, but it could be from the barbed wire they tore through. If they got one, they must have run to gut it somewhere else. I looked around for brass. Guessing it's still rolling around in their rigs."

My dog seemed to be listening to Horsmon's voice. His ears were cocked, and he was staring at the phone with that empathetic golden-retriever look that defines the breed. He seemed to know that something was wrong. He'd been my wife's pup.

"Where's Armbruster?" I asked.

Mark Armbruster was the other officer who lived in Challis, and the Pahsimeroi was part of his patrol area.

"Shit if I know. He was told to park his rig. Too much comp time."

I didn't need to ask for details. In Armbruster's absence, Horsmon was trying to cover two patrol areas, which meant he had an area roughly the state of Delaware.

"Was this yesterday?" I asked.

"The shooting was this morning. I found their camp this afternoon along Patterson Creek. It looks like they're living there. They've got four moldy camp trailers on blocks, and there's garbage everywhere. Couple of empty whiskey bottles were laying by a cold campfire and the place smells like human shit."

"What'd they have to say?"

"There wasn't anybody there and no plates on the trailers. I don't know who they are."

"Any meat hanging?"

"None. It'd spoil in this heat anyway."

I could understand why Merritt was upset. To a lot of Idahoans, elk are revered. The big animals symbolize the Rockies like bison had once done for the plains. They're wild and where they bed in the grassy meadows, they leave a mustiness that reminds me of bruised apples.

Chasing elk through a barbed-wire fence while shooting from a pickup truck was about as low as a human could ethically get with wildlife—not to mention the illegality of it. But without a witness who could identify the shooters and vehicles, these people were never going to stand in front of a judge and explain their behavior.

"Any idea how long they're gonna be around?"

"You're not listening. I think they're living there."

# Chapter 2

Merritt Horsmon is well mannered and soft spoken. He hadn't asked for help, and I think it was because he didn't know what my current caseload was. For all he knew, I had a pending trial that I was cramming for, and he didn't want to put me in a spot. It's the way Horsmon is. But he does know how to get things done. He had thrown the bait out and knew that if I could squeeze another case onto my pile, I'd surely grab it like a cutthroat taking a grasshopper.

Horsmon is one of 76 patrol officers in Idaho charged with protecting wildlife in 83,000 square miles. Thus, each Idaho Conservation Officer is responsible for handling wildlife issues over an area of a thousand square miles. Although these colossal districts are called patrol areas, the name is a throwback to bygone days when a warden would pause at the end of his driveway, look right and left and make a decision on which direction to patrol. By 1990, those days were as rare as penguins in Alaska.

Two trends changed this. First, the number of calls-for-service, which are requests for an officer, had grossly increased. These calls range from a landowner with deer eating crops, to a headless elk carcass with a bullet hole in its guts, or any other issue involving wildlife. Secondly, the face of the violator had changed. Poachers had morphed from hungry peasants who stole the king's deer for food to self-centered people searching for instant gratification.

In my grandfather's day, antlers were commonly left on the hill "cause you can't eat them," as he'd told me. Shed antlers were something to marvel at and leave for the porcupines. That's changed. An animal with large antlers (or horns) is a grossly tempting target for poachers. The bigger the better. With other wildlife crooks, it's frequently the number of animals they've killed. But whether it's the numbers on a tape measure stretched between a dead animal's antlers or the numbers of their kills, it's their ego that drives this slaughter.

One September day, I got a call from an irate hunter who had watched a kid shoot an antelope and leave it. He said there was an adult with the shooter. They had driven to the dead antelope and looked at it from the driver's window. After a few minutes, they left without getting out of the truck. The witness managed to get a license plate. When it shook out, the father told me that when he saw how small the horns were, he told his son he'd find him a bigger one. That's the face of today's poacher.

But don't get me wrong. I'm not describing American sportsmen—I'm talking about poachers.

I had spent fifteen years as a uniform patrol officer and knew Horsmon's frustration all too well. At times the job felt impossible. It was like trying to save a sinking ship by bailing with a coffee cup. For twenty-four hours a day, I was either chasing calls or within reach of the phone and available to respond. It wasn't shift work. In my entire career, I knew only two officers who had been paid overtime. Instead, we were given compensation time for anything over forty hours. Comp time was time-off. Most of the wardens I worked with dumb-downed their hours. If they didn't, their bosses would tell them to park their truck and burn time. There were just too many calls and crimes and for the most part, days of heading out on a patrol were rare.

My uniform had been hanging in the closet for three years. I'd put it away to accept a newly created Regional Investigator position. The RI job was a plain-clothes detective assignment that came with an unmarked truck. As Enforcement Chief Jon Heggen had explained the position, "just go out and investigate stuff." For me, it had sounded like an escape from the chaos of running in two directions and a blessing from Boise to focus on what I liked best— chasing wildlife thieves. It turned out I was wrong about leaving the havoc; it was a different kind of bedlam.

When I accepted the job, it was the first of such seven positions that were assigned to the regional offices. Boise had recognized that the uniform officers didn't have the time for complex cases that involved numerous players or the underground sale of wildlife. Some of the officers weren't well versed with writing search warrant affidavits and there was a growing demand for dealing with electronic evidence such as computers and cell phones. Wildlife crime fighting had gotten complicated. The uniform officers needed investigative support, and Boise felt the solution was the RI position.

When I agreed to take the job, my patrol area had been the river corridor along the Middle Fork of the Salmon River and the roadless stretch of the main Salmon River. Combined, the two river sections consisted of a hundred and fifty miles of backcountry laced by horse trails, a handful of canyon-bottom airstrips and lots of serious whitewater. It had been a young man's dream in country that was as wild as anything south of Canada. It was also territory that was wintered-in from November through March. Thus for about five months out of the year, I had to find cases on my neighboring officer's patrol areas without making them feel like I'd either stolen something from them or left them with a mess. Most of the time I managed to pull it off.

# *Chapter 3*

The following afternoon, I turned off the highway and onto the Pahsimeroi Road at Ellis. If you look up Ellis on Wikipedia, it's listed as an "unincorporated village," and that's a stretch. Google it and you'll find it has a population of 30. There are no stores, bars, gas stations or homes. It's a post office with a dirt parking lot that sits beside the highway with not another building in sight. I don't think I've ever seen more than three rigs parked at Ellis.

After a quarter mile, I was once-again struck by the pull of the Pahsimeroi. It's big, lonely country. The sagebrush valley floor is flanked by two boney mountain ranges. Both of these–the Lemhi Mountains to the east and the Big Lost Mountains to the west–have peaks that push through 11,000'. The valley is split down the middle by a small twisting river, banded by cottonwoods. The drainage is about fifty miles long and ten miles wide, and is dotted with fields of emerald green alfalfa. The glaciated peaks and cirques in the headwaters are so impressive they're called Little Switzerland. If residents–and there's only a few–want something from Walmart, it's a three-hour drive.

The name Pahsimeroi is from a spot in the valley the Shoshone people have considered sacred for thousands of years. It's a series of springs twenty-five miles up the valley that feed a small forest of lodgepole. Today it's called the Pines, and is owned by a person of wealth with a 7,000' private runway for his jet.

On the east side, the county road is paved and dotted with potholes and waffled jackrabbits. In mid-day, one can eat a sandwich sitting in the middle of the asphalt and not be disturbed by traffic. Ranches are scattered along the road, but you'll get sore feet walking between them. Unlike the Pines, most of these ranches are second and third generation family operations run on shoestrings and recycled baling twine. There are no bunkhouses or cook shacks filled with cowboys like in the movies. Occasionally you'll find a Hispanic helping with the irrigation and haying. The road on the west side is called the Custer County Road. It turns from pavement to dirt about halfway up the valley and is even lonelier than the road on the Lemhi County side.

I had hitched my personal camp trailer to my unmarked state-issued pickup truck. The little teardrop-shaped camper is a bed-on-wheels that's just tall enough to crawl into and lay on the mattress. There's a hatch in the back which opens like a car's trunk and exposes a small kitchen. Since the trailer is only five feet tall, it's the perfect rig to stash in the brush. For work trips, I'd nicknamed it my One-Man Mobile Command Post.

My job as a Regional Investigator consisted of activities that could be separated into two boxes. The first was exactly what you'd expect, the investigation of wildlife crimes with the goal of putting together a prosecutable case. The second was foggier. It involved turning information gained from informants, taxidermy logs, social media, undercover contacts and a pile of other sources into intel. And that's just a fancy word for useable information. I'd use intel to either start an investigation or file for a future project. This trip was just that—an attempt to gain intel on what was going on in the Pahsimeroi.

In talking with Horsmon, it sounded like there could have been several laws broken: hunting with vehicles, trespassing, and perhaps the subsequent killing of an elk with the aid of a vehicle. Unfortunately, the information was observed from over a mile a way. At that distance, the witness couldn't have seen elk or identified the vehicle makes or models, so this information had little evidentiary value. Horsmon had found blood and torn barbed wire. Thus there wasn't a case without another witness or a dead elk. To boot, if we ever found one, we'd have to prove it had been killed illegally.

*If it walks like a duck and quacks like a duck, it's a duck.* That's what on old game warden had told me about poachers when I was younger. I had found it to be true. What had grabbed me with Horsmon's call was that whatever this witness had *believed* he had seen in the distance, it had disturbed him enough that he'd made the call. With this fact in mind and what Horsmon had told me about the camp, my gut said there was a high probability that there was trouble in the Pahsimeroi. And besides, we owed it to both the elk and caller to follow up on his information.

Along the east side of the valley, the Lemhi Mountains rise like a mile-high wall. Twenty miles up from Ellis, there's a spot at the base of the Lemhis where the town of Patterson once thrived. Nobody lives in there anymore, but it's still home to a two-room school that serves a dozen kids. Just past the turnoff to the school, there's an old galvanized mailbox on a wooden post that sits in front of a broken-down cinderblock building with two empty garages. My granddad would have called it a filling station, and that's the only building left from the old days. Past the mail stop, there's a cut in the mountains where a creek tumbles and flows into the sagebrush flats to the Pahsimeroi River. Its course is marked by cottonwoods. They shimmer in the breeze that blows up the valley in the day and down at night.

Just across the creek at Patterson, there's a white desert the size of three or four football fields that is devoid of vegetation. It's made of finely ground mine tailings that date back from when the town had been a watering hole for hard-rock miners. These men had mucked tungsten and galena ores out of shafts and adits that they'd burrowed into the canyon with muscle and sweat. The ore had been processed in a mill up the canyon and the tailings dumped in the flat like a fallen-down tombstone.

Horsmon had said the camp was in the flat, tucked down along this creek. I slowed as I passed the turnoff and saw a mishmash of rotting camp trailers and vehicles parked near a tiny cabin a couple of hundred yards off to my right. My eye caught a puff of smoke from the center of the cluster. I continued up the county road for about a mile and found the two-track I was looking for. Three hundred yards down, I located a patch of four-foot tall sagebrush where I had previously camped on another case. It took me a few minutes to unhitch my teardrop and get it situated.

The spicy-bitter smell of sagebrush hung in the air. It was good to be back in the Pahsimeroi.

The quick look-see hadn't bought me anything other than the fact that it looked as though someone was in the camp. The sun was about four fingers above the Big Lost Range and I guessed I had two hours of daylight. I topped off Nick's bowl with dog food and pulled a box of fried chicken from the cooler. I sat down on the tailgate with a piece of chicken and thought about my options. There'd been a breeze up the valley, but it had died down and the heat from the sun was taking over. I looked across the top of the sage shining in the sun and thought about the case. I could see a dust trail from a vehicle on the other side of the valley.

Before I had left Salmon, I had gone through a three-inch stack of folders. These were my open cases. One nagged at me. It seemed to be the opposite of this Pahsimeroi case. It contained a half-dozen reports written by investigators in Montana and Wisconsin. The case involved a wealthy urologist that lived in Butte. Three days a month, he worked in the hospital in Salmon. He had a long history of killing big game animals illegally. His refined tastes preferred big mule deer bucks and bighorn sheep. Montana had revoked his license, but he had bragged that it hadn't stopped his hunting and was using other people's permits to cover his kills. The reports didn't name their sources, but it appeared they had managed to corroborate the information. Because of the Interstate Compact, his Montana revocation also prevented him from legally hunting in Idaho. I had run his name through our license database and found no evidence that he'd purchased permits, which would have been a violation.

The doctor's *modus operandi* revolved around his trophy room. If it was worth killing, it got mounted and hung on his wall. This guy could easily have dropped off a buck or ram in Salmon with one of the local head-stuffers and covered it by using somebody else's tag. I had added a taxidermist check to my mental to-do list.

I pulled another piece of chicken out the box and got my head back in the game. Most of what I did as an investigator was the same thing I had watched Joe Friday do on the Dragnet television series when I was a kid—pull the badge wallet, roll the gold, and try to find some truth between the lies and claims of chastity. But knocking on this camp's door wouldn't work, since I didn't have enough information to know what questions to ask.

For most of my career, I had been assigned long-term undercover assignments around the state. These were cases that had been developed from information from patrol officers or other sources and turned over to Boise. Headquarters would prioritize them and try to find the right officer to work the case. These assignments involved periodic trips across the state in an attempt to gain the target's confidence and could easily take a year or two of covert work for the case to come to fruition. For safety concerns, the officers selected for these roles were those who had never worked the area in uniform.

With this in my past, I was toying with either driving into the camp looking like a hunter, asking about elk, or sneaking through the brush and eyeballing it with binoculars. Neither appealed to me. A cold undercover contact without a pretext would beg for suspicion. To further complicate that option, I had worked the Pahsimeroi in uniform and most of the ranchers in the valley knew me, so walking into a camp without knowing who was there was dumb. And sitting in the brush on a hot day watching campers camp didn't sound fun or productive.

And then the echo of a rifle shot bounced off the Lemhi Range.

# *Chapter 4*

In the Rocky Mountains, elk hunting is part of the culture. Sets of elk antlers are displayed on overhead gates and restaurant walls like coats of arms. Elk meat fills the freezers and some folks swear it tastes better than beef. In September, camouflage ball caps and shirts appear. Men talk about their favorite rifle and what powder and bullets they use in their hand-loaded cartridges. By October, camp trailers and canvas wall tents appear in spots that have been used as base camps by families and friends for three or four generations. If you drag a boot heel in these camps, you'll find tiny stone chips that are about the size of a baby's fingernail. These lithic flakes were left from indigenous people who sat in these spots for thousands of years making arrowheads and atlatl dart points for elk and anything else that crossed their paths.

Most hunters purchase a *general bull tag* that allows them to start hunting an antlered elk on October 15 and runs into November. This general tag doesn't allow the hunter to harvest a cow or calf.

Killing a bull elk in the high basins of the Rockies is difficult. The country is rugged and the animals have extraordinary senses that have evolved over twenty-five million years. Elk bed in bands, ranging from a handful to over a hundred. Each of their heads will be up with ears moving like skinny brown radar domes. If they hear a footstep, they'll be up and moving. If the breeze brings the wrong scent, they're gone. Only about twelve percent of the hunters manage to harvest a bull in the general season.

Elk are big, and they seem to get bigger when they're dead. When a hunter has a bull down in the mountains, he or she has a serious problem. If it's in the bottom of a canyon, the hunter is going to call the place a hellhole before it's loaded in his truck.

The first task a hunter faces with a downed bull is the removal of the internal organs, which are comprised of the intestinal tract, kidneys, liver, bladder, lungs and heart. Collectively, hunters call these guts, so the act of removing them is called gutting. It's difficult to gut an elk that's facing downhill, since the organs weigh roughly eighty pounds and act like a heavy wet blob. It's much easier to remove the organs if the head is uphill, since gravity helps pull them. But rotating an elk that weighs 700 pounds is tough and sometimes nearly impossible for one person to accomplish if rocks or downed trees are in the way.

The intimidating challenge isn't the gutting, but getting the elk to a truck and loaded. Some folks will joke about carrying a fork so they can eat the animal where it died. If the hunter has a friend with pack horses or mules, packsaddles, and the needed packing skills, the animals can be walked in to the kill site the following day. The carcass needs to be skinned and quartered. Each quarter has to be lifted and tied to one side of a pack animal and then secured with a barrel or basket hitch. Most hunters don't have horses and more than likely, they'll have to resort to pack frames and brute strength. A bull's two front quarters will weigh a hundred pounds apiece and each hindquarter will weigh about seventy-five pounds. The fourth quarter always weighs more than the first. It's not a job for old men.

The Idaho Fish and Game divides the State into seven geographic regions. I was assigned to the Salmon Region, which is over 8,000 square miles in the central part of the State and home to the River of No Return—better known as the Salmon River. About 95 percent of the region is federal ground, administered by the Bureau of Land Management and the Forest Service.

Roughly five percent of the region is comprised of agricultural land. It's almost exclusively used for what's called cow-calf ranching. It's a simple agricultural concept. The rancher's cows produce calves that are sold in the fall. The adult cows produce another crop of fresh calves in late winter. When the snow is gone and the vegetation has greened up, the cow-calf pairs are moved to public ground in the mountains. In October, the herds are brought back to the ranch and are fed baled alfalfa, which is raised on the ranch in the summer.

A normal day for a rancher, from one season to the next, might include dealing with freshly birthed calves in a blizzard, moving cows on government ground from horseback, irrigating alfalfa, cutting hay, fixing fence and a hundred other less-categorized chores. A well-worked cow-calf operation is not a job for the lazy. If a rancher takes a day off, something isn't getting done.

Both elk and cattle are hoofed animals that eat grasses and forbs, but that's about all they have in common. If you look at a beef cow from the rear, they have short legs and a torso shaped like a barrel. An elk's torso is laterally compressed and their legs are long. The front of their shins are sheathed with quarter-inch thick skin that protects them while sprinting through jungles of downed timber. The large bulls with nearly five-foot long antlers can lift their chins and charge through dog hair lodgepole like antelope in the sage. Elk are graceful and built to move.

In early summer, elk compete with cattle for feed on public ground. If it's a dry year, the grasses cure out by the middle of July, which causes an odd interchange that is similar to Mark Twain's *The Prince and the Pauper*. Elk move down to the lush irrigated private ground while the landowner's cattle are confined by barbed wire to the dry feed on public land. With tens of thousands of elk in the state, conflicts between elk and agriculture are common, and a landowner finding seventy-five head of elk in his alfalfa has a problem.

Historically, farmers dominated the Idaho legislature and that legacy lives on; the agricultural industry has tremendous political clout in the state. The legislators have made it clear to the Fish and Game Department that when wildlife becomes a problem for a farmer, they will find a solution or issue a check for damages out of their already skinny budget.

When Horsmon had called, it was the second day of a sixty-day elk hunt that started the first of August. This hunt is very different than the general bull hunt. A person can buy a tag to hunt an antlerless elk–cows and calves–as long as they are within a mile of a cultivated field. The department's biologists had developed this hunt to respond to complaints from ranchers who had problems with late-summer elk. On its face, these hunts are a solution to elk depredating in alfalfa fields at night and spending their days hiding in the nearby sagebrush hills and creek bottoms. Hunters can attempt long stalks by concealing themselves behind terrain or vegetation. Or they try an ambush after patterning the animal's movements. It's an endeavor that takes skill and effort and with a fair amount of luck, works for the hunter. In theory, the pressure pushes the elk back to the high country and placates the landowners and the legislators. In theory.

There are two problems with these valley hunts; first, the elk seldom choose to quit the lush feed and secondly, these hunts attract unethical hunters like flies to garbage.

# *Chapter 5*

The roar of the rifle shot had jolted me into a focus as if I'd been slapped. Standing in the bed of the truck, I rested my elbows on the cab and studied the direction it had come from through a pair of binoculars. By following the edge of the mountains, I located a light-colored vehicle about a mile away that looked like it was stopped next to an alfalfa field. Heat waves twisted and blurred whatever was happening.

I told Nick to kennel. He jumped into the truck bed, sensing that something was up. I closed the tailgate and threw my box of chicken on the passenger seat. I put a camouflage ball cap on. It took me a few minutes to get to the county road. As I approached the vehicle, I slowed and pulled a piece of chicken out of the box.

It was an old dented Econoline van painted two shades of white, with a plate from southern Idaho. It was stopped in the northbound lane with two people staring at me through a cracked and bug spattered windshield. I pulled next to the driver's window and took a bite of chicken. The driver looked like he was pushing fourteen and his passenger was even younger. The younger one cradled a rifle between his knees. Its blued barrel was in front of his face. Both looked like they had their fingers in the cookie jar.

"I'm hunting elk," I said with a mouthful of chicken. "You guys seen any?"

The driver replied in a husky voice, "We're elk huntin' too."

The passenger hollered, "I just got me a jackrabbit."

I asked if they wanted a piece of chicken. The driver looked at the passenger and whispered something to him. The younger kid leaned over and set something on the floor. I got out with a couple of drumsticks in a paper towel and handed them through the window. The driver put his arm over a beverage can in his crotch and I thought I could smell beer on his breath. His teeth were yellow and crooked and neither of them were using their seatbelts.

"Camped around here?" I asked.

The driver looked towards Patterson and held the drumstick to his mouth with dirty fingers. "Down on the creek."

"Seen any elk?"

The driver's crooked teeth flashed. "We got some a couple nights ago."

"You kidding me?" I asked.

"Shit no," he bragged. "Our dad gets more damn elk than anybody." Again he nodded towards the camp. "Go talk to him. He'll tell you every damn thing you wanna know about huntin'."

"What's his name?" I asked.

"Jerry."

I thanked the two and watched in the mirror as the boys drove towards Patterson. A freshly killed jackrabbit lay in a pool of blood where the van had stopped. The older boy looked too young to have a driver's license and his passenger looked too young to have a hunting license. I was convinced I had just stumbled onto a couple of juveniles drinking, driving, and shooting from the road.

I thought about my badge wallet and magnetic blue light stashed behind the seat in a duffel bag. I'd taken all of my enforcement gear and hidden it in the bag in case I decided to drive into the camp posing as a hunter. I flipped a coin in my brain and decided to let the kids go. It bothered me.

# *Chapter 6*

I had been using the name Pisano. It had belonged to my late wife, whom I dearly loved.

For some curious reason, officers who work undercover frequently select the surname of a person they respect for their cover name. It's usually a relative that has passed. This practice isn't something that is suggested in training or handed from one operator to the next. I think it's a simple gut response from a human who misses another. It just happens.

The first cover name I used was Henderson. I had borrowed it from my grandparents. When I rode a red Huffy and packed a fully loaded cap gun, they lived ten minutes away and I spent a lot of time at their house. We were tight–I told them stories my parents never heard.

When my Henderson cover became too well known, I took my grandmother's maiden name of Hill. As Tony Hill, I wore a black NRA ball cap, a weeklong beard and dirty jeans. I looked the part. When I put that hat on and became Hill, I felt like an outlaw and enjoyed it a bit too much.

I hadn't over-used the Hill cover, but when my wife passed, I had an urge to use her name and not let her go. I felt that in some mystic fashion, she would still be there and perhaps watch my back. At least that's what I had hoped. She'd been dead for over a year. I'm sure this was a puzzling attempt to help me deal with the black hole of grief.

\*\*\*\*\*

After watching the boys drive away in their van, I headed back to my teardrop, dropped the tailgate, let Nick out and poured a quart of water into his bowl. I pulled a camouflage shirt out of the camper, put it on, and made sure nothing looked amiss inside the cab of the truck. Pulling my elk rifle out of its case, I rested the muzzle on the truck's floor and leaned its green fiberglass stock on the seat. A box of shells and a hunting knife on the dash completed the scene.

When I hit the county road, I turned towards Patterson and soon found an empty Budweiser can lying in the southbound lane like an orphaned glove. It hadn't been there when I had driven up from Ellis. I stopped and threw it in the back of the truck. Nick sniffed it for a moment and crawled back into his padded dog box.

Crossing the creek, I turned down the dirt road in front of the old filling station and studied the camp for a moment. I could see a handful of people sitting in chairs. The white van was parked a couple hundred yards off to the north in front of the Patterson school and the two boys were playing. The younger one was sitting in a swing set rocking back and forth. The older one looked like he was throwing rocks.

My immediate mission was to try to find out who was in the camp, sniff out the dominant dog, and get a feel for what they were up to.

Had this been an overt contact with a badge, I would have been carrying an audio recorder, but I had been patted down for a wire in a bar in Idaho Falls, so I had nothing on me–including a sidearm that would burn me.

The place didn't look like an elk camp; it looked like a lived-in ghetto. Four old camp trailers and a faded motor home were parked helter-skelter near a small log cabin. The cabin's logs needed oil and its door was propped open with a big cobble. Black plastic garbage bags were stuffed and piled near the trailers. An antique International Harvester crew cab with an Idaho plate was parked next to a newer black Dodge pickup wearing an Arkansas plate. I verbalized the plates to myself in an attempt to memorize them.

Three adult females sat in camp chairs smoking cigarettes. Two looked like they were a mother-daughter pair. The third was odd. She was in her twenties with pale skin. Her long black hair was balding and exposed most of her shiny scalp. A fourth woman walked out of the cottonwoods with a roll of toilet paper and stepped into the cabin. Two men wearing ball caps were leaning on a nearby gold colored GMC pickup. The older one was holding a can of Budweiser, and a cigarette dangled from his lips. Both were staring at me.

It truly seemed like Appalachia.

I scanned everyone's face again. Nobody looked familiar. I took a breath, stepped out of the truck and told Nick to stay put. It was show time.

Looking at the two men by the GMC, I raised my hand. "Hey," and nodded towards the school. "Those kids said I should talk to somebody here about elk hunting. Said his name was Jerry."

   The man with the beer walked over, took a drag on his cigarette and pulled it away from his lips. "Those are my boys," he said smiling. "I'm Jerry."

# Chapter 7

Jerry and I were standing near my pickup. Nick was watching us from the bed. The woman I had seen with the toilet paper came over and stepped between us like a horse to a grain bucket. She was in her mid-thirties and too raunchy to be called attractive. Her shoulder-length sandy hair hadn't seen shampoo for a while, and her peach lipstick was smudged. She held a glass full of ice cubes and what looked like whiskey. Her camouflage halter-top pulled her fake boobs into a deep and tanned valley. Her denim shorts had been cut off to allow the pocket liners to hang below the ragged edge. To top it off, her tan legs were stuck in a pair of red cowboy boots.

She reached up towards Nick and asked, "What's your dog's name?"

Her question had come out sounding as if she had a grape under her tongue. I couldn't tell if she was drunk or had a southern accent or both.

I shook my head. "He's psycho. Doesn't like petting." I had just told these people my first lie—I didn't want any of this crew getting near my late wife's dog.

The woman jerked her hand back, took another step towards me, and lifted her glass. "You wanna have a drink, or something else?" Her eyes were smiling and I had the distinct impression I'd been offered a joint.

Things were getting uncomfortable.

Jerry interceded and turned to her. "Tell Leroy we're gonna go for a drive in a half-hour." It wasn't a request.

Parting her lips, she rattled the ice cubes and said, "You get dry, I'll fix you up." She turned and walked away with a smooth elastic gait, her hips rolling like a catwalk model.

Jerry and I watched her move towards the fire ring. When she was out of hearing, he said, "That's Trixie. She's with Leroy."

He'd said it in an absolute way. It was a one-sided conversation that was over. The dominant dog had just warned me that she was off-limits. I smiled to myself, for I had just found the guy with the keys to the car.

Jerry took another pull on his cigarette. His head reminded me of a pit bull, flat and wide. His forearms were wiry and tanned; his hands were abraded and calloused. Whatever he did for a living didn't happen behind a desk— he looked strong. He was just short of six feet and looked to be in his late forties, but I figured he was younger. His light green eyes looked like they belonged to a lizard and were set off by deep wrinkles. His tanned cheeks hadn't seen a razor for a week or two. The bill on his yellow ball cap was dirty from being grabbed with greasy fingers. What I could see of his hair was dark and oily and needed a barber. Like his sons, he had crooked yellow teeth, but was missing an upper canine.

"Your kid said you're hunting elk. You seeing any?"

He smirked and nodded. "It's good up here. We been doing this hunt the last three years. You just drive down the road and dump 'em right in the middle, load 'em up and go gut 'em in the sagebrush." His grin got bigger and his eyes got darker. "Last year I killed eleven. The year before we shot thirteen of the fuckers."

I tried not to blink.

His kids drove by in the van. He waved and flicked his cigarette into the dry sage.

"We own this ground."

Movement by the fire ring caught my eye. I glanced over while my brain tried to wrap around the elk numbers he had just claimed. The young female with the balding head was standing with a beer in her hand. She was thin, but grossly pregnant as if she were concealing a melon under her pink top. She stared at me and her expressionless face was frozen like a bad painting.

Jerry saw my gaze. "That's my dad's wife."

"Looks like you're gonna have a little brother."

He sniggered. "No, she's always looked like that. Looked like that when she was fifteen."

I brought the subject back. "If you don't mind me asking, where you finding these elk?"

He took a pull from his Budweiser and looked up the valley where I had talked to his kids. "The fuckers cross the road right up there," he said and lifted his chin. "Lay you're rifle on the hood and shoot. You can get 'em right on the highway."

"Where you guys from?" I asked. "I'm from Hailey."

"Blackfoot." He glanced into the open door of my truck. "What you shootin'?"

"Thirty-five Whelen," I said. "Shoots a 250 grain slug."

"This is what you need." He walked over to his truck and pulled a scoped rifle out that had a black plastic stock. "Three Hundred Winchester Magnum. Shoots as flat as my ass."

As he'd said this, Jerry had carelessly swung the muzzle by the guy he'd been talking with. I noticed this guy's eyes were drilling through me. He had a goatee made from a dozen hairs. His cheeks were covered with acne scars. His ball cap was crooked and crunched down, and his ears stuck out at odd angles.

Jerry held the rifle out and I took it. The bolt was cocked and the safety was set. I assumed there was a round in the chamber. I brought it up to my shoulder keeping my finger out of the trigger guard and looked through the scope focusing on a distant cottonwood. "This puppy'll reach out and touch something, eh?"

"A thousand yards and knock the shit out of the fuckers."

I brought it back down and examined it. It was a Howa with a cheap 3-9 variable powered scope.

As I handed it back to him, two shots rang out from up the valley.

Jerry looked towards the shooting. "My boys have a good time up here."

I cocked my head and raised my voice, "You think they're into elk?"

"Just killin' jacks. They ain't good for nuthin'. Rez dogs'll starve on 'em."

The mention of the reservation caught my ear and I wondered if Jerry was a tribal member. Blackfoot was on the edge of the Fort Hall Reservation. If he was an Indian that resided on the reservation, it would make an investigation and prosecution complex, but not impossible. For a second, I was tempted to ask him, but I decided to let it go–I couldn't let this conversation sound like an interrogation. Especially with this other player who was listening and still staring at me.

"So I should just drive the roads?"

Jerry nodded. "Yeah, you might see us out there tonight."

I thanked him and got in my truck. As I turned around, I noted his license plate, held my breath for a moment and then quietly vocalized the numbers twice to get it in my brain.

I blinked and took a breath. Jerry's statement of killing eleven elk the previous year and being a party to the killing of thirteen elk the year before was buzzing around my brain like a horsefly. The other thing was what his kid had said, "We got some the other night" and yet Jerry hadn't brought it up. Why had he bragged about killing so many the last two years, but not boasted about what they'd done this year? Could it be that his kids were talking about spotlighting elk and Jerry was keeping it quiet? It had been an enlightening few minutes and I knew I had been in a duck pond.

Most serious poachers in North America are driven by their egos. As I said before, it's about the numbers. Jerry and the Montana doctor were both of this ilk. The doctor had his rows of trophy mounts, each with their Boone and Crocket scores hung in his trophy house for his dinner guests to ooh-and-ah over. Jerry had his dead-elk numbers. With twenty-four dead elk in two years, he could sit on any bar stool in America and repeat those numbers and feel the flush like he was sucking a shot of tequila.

On its face, what Jerry had said was a boast, but how much of it was true? I'd known a few crooks that never lied about the numbers, probably because they didn't have to. Even if Jerry had doubled his real numbers, anything over one elk would have been illegal. And then there was the talk about shooting from the road, which hadn't sounded like bragging and was what Horsmon's witness said he'd seen.

What burned me, though, was that not once during the conversation had he called these superb animals elk. He'd called them fuckers.

Twenty-four elk in two years. What was he doing with them? We hadn't had reports of elk shot and left in the Pahsimeroi. Was he selling the meat or giving it away? And how would a guy get that many tags to launder that many elk? In Idaho, the only person that could legally tag an elk was the one who killed it. With what I had seen and what Jerry had said, there could be as many as a half-dozen elk tags in this camp. There was also the possibility that when an elk was down, he'd get on the phone and somebody would buy a tag and haul-butt for Patterson. I'd seen it before.

Beyond all the talk of dead elk, the hand that was squeezing my gut belonged to the guy who had been ogling me. He had stared like he was watching a bad movie he couldn't turn off. Had he recognized me?

I drove back up the valley, searching for a cell phone signal so I could unload on Horsmon. Not finding any, I took a dirt road that cut across to the other side and parked on a high point. Against the department's rules, I put Nick in the cab, rolled my window down, and listened for shots.

The air was dead calm and smelled of alkaline dust and sagebrush.

After a half-hour, I caught something moving along the edge of the river bottom and I brought my binoculars up. A cow and calf elk had moved out of the cottonwoods and were looking towards an alfalfa field a quarter of a mile away. Between the thick bottoms where they stood and the field lay a flat plain with short sagebrush that wouldn't hide their shins.

Three more elk appeared behind them. I stepped out of the truck to avoid the distortion of the windshield. The new group consisted of two cows and another calf. After looking around, they bumped up to the first two and stopped. The lead cow looked back into the trees and a spiked bull with foot-long velvet antlers joined them. His year-old body was smaller than the adult cows and his flanks were a lighter tan, almost yellow compared to the females. The lowering sunlight made them look like they were on fire. All six stared towards the hayfield and looked as nervous as mice in a snake's cage. After five minutes of studying the field they turned and disappeared back into the cottonwoods.

My back was towards the Big Lost Range. I was facing east towards the valley and the Lemhi Range. Behind me, the sun dipped below the mountains. The breeze quit and the mood from the sage came into my truck like a dream. I watched a dark shadow walk across the Pahsimeroi. When it touched the edge of the Lemhis, it seemed to pause and then it marched to the top. Halfway to Ellis, a lonely yard light flickered and came on.

Bringing my binoculars up, I soon found two sets of taillights working slowly down the far side of the valley towards Patterson. After about three miles, the first vehicle paused and then a shot rolled across the plain.

It was past legal shooting hours. I started the engine and drove with my lights off, relying on the twilight until I crossed the river and flicked them on. When I got to the stretch of road where the vehicles had been, there wasn't a soul. My headlights found a dead jackrabbit lying on the asphalt. I stepped out and looked. Wisps of steam came off its cactus-colored guts that had been jerked and twisted by the bullet.

I turned my truck off, felt the cool air settling into the valley and listened to the engine ping. After twenty minutes, the darkness had fully covered the Pahsimeroi. When I was satisfied nothing was moving, I drove past the Patterson town site and looked down along the creek. A large fire was roaring in the camp and four-foot flames lit the place up. Several people were standing around with drinks in their hands. Their faces glowed and they swayed back and forth like they were worshipping a god I hadn't met.

# Chapter 8

The following morning, I managed to get my teardrop down the valley and past Ellis without coming across any of the camp's vehicles. I had to drive nearly sixty miles along the Salmon River before I hit cell service. On the first attempt, Horsmon picked up and I started my regurgitation.

When I was done, he spoke his in his soft voice, "Told you so."

After I didn't respond, he asked, "Now what are you gonna do?"

I didn't have an answer. What I did know was there's a ratio for undercover work that's about 1:5. For every hour you're *under* there's at least another five hours of follow-up work. Granted, I was only undercover for thirty minutes, but I had work to do.

When I got home, I logged into the state vehicle database and ran the two resident plates. The old International Harvester came back to a 1968 Travelall registered to Claude Dowling of Blackfoot. His birth date put him at sixty-nine, and I suspected he was Jerry's dad. The gold GMC came back to Gerald Dowling, also of Blackfoot, age forty. I scratched my head, looked at the height and weight, and thought about Jerry's sun-beaten face. I decided that this was probably him. But could Claude, at sixty-nine, be wedded to a balding twentyish wife?

I logged onto the Fish and Game license database and ran the two names. Both had elk tags for the Pahsimeroi that were valid for the green-field hunt.

To run the Arkansas plate, I drove to the Lemhi County Sheriff's office and asked the dispatcher to enter it in their nationwide system. The black Dodge came back to a Leroy Barnes, of Flippin, Arkansas. Like Gerald Dowling, he too was forty.

The dispatcher ran all three names for driver's licenses. Barnes' name didn't come back through the Arkansas database. I had her run him through Idaho and got a hit showing a Blackfoot address. While I was pondering that information, I heard the dispatcher say, "Two of these guys have records. I'll print them for you."

While the dot matrix was spitting out a sheet longer than my leg, I looked at Barnes' address he'd given for his driver's license and discovered it was the same address that Gerald Dowling had claimed.

I pulled the roll off the printer. The first record belonged to Claude Dowling. His initial felony had been a burglary ten months after his eighteenth birthday. Since juvenile crimes are sealed, the record didn't show anything before that first arrest. Two years later, he was nailed with three more counts of burglary. And four years after that, he'd been convicted of forging checks. His last conviction was when he was forty-two. He'd raped a minor child and was sentenced to prison for ten years.

I thought about the pregnant-looking woman who Jerry had said was his father's wife. When I'd mentioned her appearance, he had laughed and said, "she'd looked like that since she was fifteen." Wondering if this balding woman had been Claude Dowling's child-rape victim, I did the math and couldn't get it to pencil out. Claude's young wife had been born after his discharge.

Gerald Dowling's record was longer and started off with a domestic battery when he was twenty. Within a year, he had been convicted of a burglary, followed by a list of several DUIs that I didn't bother to count. Associated with one of those was a felony eluding that put him in the same penitentiary that his father had done time in. After that first jolt, Dowling pulled off a felony DUI and drew a sentence for two more years. I counted eight times he been cited for driving without a seatbelt. There were six charges for driving without privileges. A handful of battery charges peppered his record.

Studying the timeline on Gerald's record, he'd made it off parole in May. That grabbed at me, since–according to him–he'd been involved in the killing of thirteen elk the fall before while still on parole, which should have precluded him from possessing a firearm.

I looked back at Claude Dowling's prison date and plugged his son's birthdate into his timeline. Claude had been incarcerated when Gerald was fifteen. Assuming Gerald had made it through high school, his father had missed his graduation while in the crowbar motel. Looking back at Gerald's history, I assumed he was already having problems with alcohol and probably hadn't been issued a cap and gown.

Leroy Barnes' criminal record came up blank in Idaho and Arkansas. I was tempted to ask the dispatcher to start running him in other states but didn't see the point.

Recalling that Dowling had mentioned, "we own this place," I thanked the dispatcher and went upstairs to the county assessor's office. I showed my credentials to the clerk and explained what I was looking for. He brought up an aerial map on his computer with plot lines. I pointed the cabin out to him and after a couple of mouse clicks, he swiveled his chair towards me and said, "The owner is Leroy Barnes."

At the mention of the name, a woman two desks over popped her head up and for a moment, she made eye contact.

I turned back to the assessor and asked for the mailing address for Barnes' tax bill. It showed the same Arkansas address as his truck registration.

Before I left the courthouse, I dropped back down the stairs to the sheriff's office and had the dispatcher run Barnes' hunting license history. It showed that he had purchased a resident hunting license and Pahsimeroi elk tag a week before in Blackfoot and he had used the same physical address as Gerald Dowling. On its face, the facts indicated Barnes had unlawfully purchased his resident license and tag. If he killed an elk, it too would be illegal.

On the way home, I questioned what I had done. There were now at least six people who knew the department had an interest in this Patterson crew. Horsmon was solid and his lips were sealed. I didn't know the dispatcher, but I assumed she would keep her mouth closed. And now there

were two people in the assessor's office who were aware of
our interest in Barnes and one of them had reacted as if she
knew him. Then there was Horsmon's witness; when your
day consists of alfalfa, fences and cows, calling the law on
outsiders is a big event and gossip flies like a bird with
ranchers. I had to assume that half the people in the
Pahsimeroi believed the Fish and Game's eyeball was on
this crew. It begged the question: how foolish would I be to
pursue Jerry Dowling as Tony Pisano?

# *Chapter 9*

So what *was* I going to do? I was certain that with a little more work, Leroy Barnes was going down for residency fraud. What I assumed he was doing was shorting the state about $500 annually. His resident elk tag and license had cost him $60. But if he hadn't been so conniving by trading in his Arkansas driver's license and lying about his address on his Idaho driver's license, the hunting license and elk tag would have cost $570. Looking back at Barnes' past license purchases, it showed that he'd been doing it for seven years. What pissed me off–assuming he was a resident of Arkansas–the statute of limitations had run out for five of those years and he was on home base with a savings of about $2500.

But all I had on Jerry Dowling were his boasts. Even if he found Jesus and showed up on Horsmon's steps to confess, it wouldn't be admissible without any corroboration and those elk were gone like Christmas past. What I needed on him was a fresh bloody case. Something more than a dust plume witnessed from a mile away.

There was still a cup of cold coffee in my carafe. I microwaved it and sat down in front of my computer. I read through the scribbled notes that I had made in the teardrop and let the scene play out in my head. I listened to his words and watched his face. I saw him suck on his cigarette and flip it into the sagebrush. The man who I believed was Gerald Dowling had swung at three pitches and missed.

Three times he'd had a chance, and three times he'd chosen to drop the F-bomb instead of the word elk.

It was at the police academy where an instructor had lectured about the ethics of criminal investigations and how it was important to avoid emotional involvement to maintain an objective perspective. I had found this to be unrealistic. I believed that if an investigator wasn't offended by the crime, the case wouldn't get the energy it deserved and the officer would end up in the doughnut shop. Dowling, with his disrespect for wildlife and boasts of crookedness, had managed to piss me off.

I cranked out a three-page report that detailed my contact with the Dowling kids and their father. It included a word-for-word rendition of the conversation I'd had in the camp, backed up with my notes, but left Trixie's red boots out. I created a folder named *Alfalfa* on my desktop and saved the report.

I sent an email off to the state police requesting driver's license photos of Barnes and both of the Dowlings.

But I was now at an impasse. I had done everything I could with the information I had gained. Somehow I needed to twist this into a prosecution beyond Barnes' residency fraud. I needed to put a stop to Dowling, assuming his claims were true.

My cell vibrated and started walking to the edge of the desk. It was Horsmon.

"Somebody trashed the Patterson School."

My head twisted. "Where'd you hear this?"

"One of the deputies here in Challis. Said they got a call from the teacher."

"What do you mean trashed?"

"He didn't say. They passed it on to Lemhi County."

I eyed my handwritten notes. "Had to be Dowling's kids. There's nobody else up there."

"Who the hell's Dowling?"

I explained the three names I had come up with and the fact that I had seen Jerry's two kids at the school.

"I've got some other crap going on in the East Fork," Horsmon said. "But I suppose I could drive around and wave the flag in the Pahsimeroi. Maybe I'll get lucky and catch them chasing elk again."

I thought about Horsmon's bachelor status and for a moment and toyed with responding with a snide comment about he and Trixie, but I took a sip of coffee. It was cold.

"I thought about us trying to watch from across the valley with spotting scopes," I said.

"You think that would gain anything?" He had said it with a twinge of doubt.

"Wouldn't hink them up like you driving around in a marked truck, but yeah, it would probably be a waste of time in that big valley."

Horsmon was asking the question without asking it again; *what are you going to do?*

I took another swallow of cold coffee. "Let me think about this thing."

After the phone call, I re-read my report and let it soak while I eyed the paragraphs and bullet points and heard Dowling's brags again. I watched his eyes move around like he was hearing voices. I saw his youngest holding the big rifle between his knees and caught the kid hiding what was probably a beer. I realized I had turned a corner.

These people from southern Idaho had chosen to poach in my backyard. It was a place I had no business working undercover. The rational course would be to put together an intelligence packet and turn it into Boise with a request that they assign the case to an undercover for next year. If it sounded promising, headquarters might be able to make it happen, but it depended on what else their mill had rolling down the conveyor belt. There was a good chance that my request wouldn't be granted for two years, and this realization rubbed me, since that would bump into my planned retirement date. This thing with Dowling and Barnes was a bad pothole. I needed to fix it before I hung it up.

I had never had a plan with this crew beyond spending the night, poking around and trying to get a sense of what was afoot. My contact with Dowling had been a spur of the moment decision catalyzed by the gunshot fired by his youngest son. I hadn't planned on working him undercover. I hadn't weighed the facts or used a logical process. I hadn't bounced it off my boss or the office of special operations in Boise. I couldn't put a finger on when I'd made the decision to try and work him. I think it was subconscious. It had probably started during Dowling's brags of F-bomb elk nudged by Barnes' fraud. All of this and the recent information of what his kids had undoubtedly done to the school had pushed me to the edge. And I had to get this case done before I retired.

# *Chapter 10*

The Golden Rule for undercover investigations is that unless an officer has a direct operational need-to-know, its existence isn't disclosed. The more people that know about its existence, the greater the chance it will be compromised.

I had already committed a dimwitted sin by doing overt work on Barnes' residency fraud while the door was still open for more covert work. Granted, the assessor's office was only aware that I had an interest in Barnes and where they were mailing his tax bill, but it hadn't been my brightest moment. I should have waited and chased the lead after I was done with any undercover work. This indiscretion may have been okay in a populated place like Boise or Seattle, but not the tiny burg of Salmon, Idaho. Everybody seems to know everybody, and it's not just those folks that live in town. The residents of Salmon know half the people in Challis, and seem to know every rancher in between and the names of their kids.

The sheriff's dispatch told me who was working the Patterson School case. I called the officer's cell and told him I knew something about his case. I had known deputy Terry Stratton for a long time. We'd backed each other up on calls for over a decade and his trust was well tested. I also knew something he didn't; we had a common interest in Patterson.

The lanky deputy met me at the sheriff's office wearing a dark blue uniform shirt, jeans and duty belt. He had a thick manila envelope in his hand and led me into an interview room. The steel door clunked and we both took chairs at a table that dominated the claustrophobic room.

We both laid our packets down. I pulled an eight by ten glossy out and rolled it like a twenty-one dealer laying down an ace of spades. It was Gerald Dowling's unsmiling driver's license photo that the state police had emailed. It wasn't flattering.

Stratton squinted and his crow's feet kicked into his temples. He growled, "Who's this asshole?"

"He's the father of the two shits who tore your school up. That's their camp you woulda seen over by the creek."

I reinforced the fact that what I was going to tell him needed to stay in the room. The whiskers in his thick western mustache tightened and he scowled. I ignored him and articulated how I had come to my conclusion that the two boys in the white van had been the ones who trashed the school.

He nodded. "The teacher thinks the same thing. She described two male juvies and said they were in a van. Said they drove by and acted like she was invisible when she waved."

Stratton's envelope was thicker than mine. He pulled out his own stack of photographs and flopped two down as if to trump my lone ace. The first photo showed a glass door that had been smashed. His second picture focused on two baseball bats lying on a dry yellowing lawn.

"That's what they used to break the safety glass to get in. Two bats, so two suspects, but I think there may have been three."

He rolled out another glossy. "This is what they did first." The photograph showed a classroom with open drawers on the back wall and scattered CD's and board games on the floor. Two of the desks were overturned and broken.

Stratton pointed to a desktop computer. "One of them tried to log onto Facebook."

"Were you able to figure out what their username was?"

Stratton shook his head and frowned. "I've got a call into the state lab. The computer guy's on vacation and I'm a retard with this stuff."

The next photograph exposed the second classroom. All of the cabinets were open and empty. Books and photographs were scattered on the floor and a pink liquid had been poured and flung about on the pile. A computer monitor had been broken and was flung cockeyed in a sink.

Stratton plunked down another glossy. It was a close up of a shoe track where somebody had stepped in the pink goo. The tread elements consisted of thick zigzagging bars. "That's a cleaning chemical they dumped."

He pulled out another photo without speaking. It was a close-up of the word "penis" written carefully in a neat, concise fashion with a heavy red felt-tipped marker on a white interior wall. The letters were crafted in a large italic font as if a computer had printed them. Who ever had written it was a good student. My head canted and I thought about my own illegible scribbles. "That looks like a female's writing."

"Exactly," he said nodding. "And a guy would have more than likely used something like cock or just drawn a dick with balls. Penis is too clinical for a guy."

Stratton's next show-and-tell was a card with clear tape on it that he'd used to lift a fingerprint. "That's the only good latent I found. It was on one of two fire extinguishers they took outside and had a war with."

"You talk to anybody in the camp?" I asked.

"I'd prefer to call it a shit hole." Stratton said. "I'm surprised one of your bears hasn't come out of the canyon and gotten in their garbage. But yeah, there was some old drunken bald-headed bastard who answered one of the trailer doors. Said he hadn't seen anybody at the school. I got the idea he was the only one in camp."

"You know anybody in that country with crooked ears and bad acne scars?"

Stratton laughed and didn't answer.

I rolled out a second glossy driver's license photo of a pudgy older male with a neck wider than his head. He was bald, with thick Elvis sideburns and a double chin.

"This guy?" I asked.

"Yeah, he was the drunk."

"He's Claude Dowling. His name will pop up as a sex-offender." I pointed at my first photo. "I think he's this guy's dad, but I haven't had the joy of meeting him yet."

Stratton shook his head. "I would have asked for ID, but all he was wearing was his whitey-tighty Fruit of the Loom's. Didn't want to have to glove up."

I produced Gerald Dowling's driver's license printout from my envelope. Stratton wrote the information on his

48

packet and said, "I'll run up there as soon as I can, but today's the end of my week. I've got two days."

I nodded. "I might be up sooner."

# *Chapter 11*

The next afternoon, Nick and I headed for the Pahsimeroi with my teardrop, another box of fried chicken and a six-pack of beer.

After hiding the little camper in the tall sage, I drove over to the Patterson camp.

The only vehicle was the faded RV that had been parked there before. I could see a man looking out the side window at me. Grabbing the brown paper sack that was sitting on my seat, I got out and walked around the rear of the vehicle. Roofing tar had been smeared along the corners and a gob had been splotched over the license plate stamp to hide the expiration date.

When I got to the passenger side, the guy was standing in the doorway. He was well over six feet and had to duck to stick his head out. His hair was black and curly and it framed his puffy cheeks. His size was intimidating.

"Is Jerry around?" I asked.

His voice was deep and hoarse like he'd been yelling. "Who's asking?" As soon as he said it, he glanced over at the school.

I stepped up the stairs and stuck out my hand. "Pisano, Tony Pisano." He'd started this game, and I was going to run with it and try to figure out who he was.

He hesitated, but finally after an awkward moment, he stuck his paw out and it felt like I was grabbing a boa constrictor. I glimpsed behind him and saw a stack of rifles leaning on a couch.

"It's Bill," he snarled. "Whatcha need with Jerry?" It came out more of a challenge than a question.

"Just wanted to thank him for his help." I held up the brown paper bag. I got into some elk."

He studied the bag like he thought I might be a process server with a ruse, but his face twitched and got sincere. "You can leave that with me. I'll make sure he gets it."

"He around or did he go home?" I asked.

He glanced up the drainage and said, "He's around. I think everybody's out hunting."

I nodded. "Good, I'll run down and give it to him. You guys having any luck?"

He snorted. "I don't do this hunt. I buy Middle Fork tags. I brought my kids up here so they can shoot an antelope."

The only open antelope season was an archery hunt. This giant—with all the rifles behind him—didn't look like the bowhunters I knew. He was wearing a dirty red muscle shirt exposing his armpits. A pair of hairy legs and bare feet stuck out of plaid pajama bottoms that were too short.

"You guys are archery hunters, eh?" I asked. "I used to pull a string when I was younger. Still got my compound."

He smiled and his eyes pinched down. "Sure, bowhunters. That's us." It was spoken with a sarcastic tone.

My face turned up the valley. "I'll find him sooner or later. Still got a tag to fill, so I'll be here for a couple of days."

I took the brown bag and headed towards my truck, wondering if he'd been watching the RV's backup camera when I had stopped to memorize his license plate.

Glancing around the camp, I looked for a baseball mitt or something to connect this hovel to the school rampage. All I caught was the acidic odor of the fire pit mixed with the smell of garbage and Bill's face staring at me from the RV's window. What I didn't see was a foam archery target that should have been there if Bill's kids were truly bowhunters.

When I got to the fallen-down filling station, I pulled a notebook out and wrote down the RV's license plate.

A vehicle approached and I realized it was the green sun baked Travelall. I rolled my window down and stuck my head out. The driver stopped and I recognized that it was Claude Dowling from his driver's license photo. The young balding woman who Jerry had said was his wife was sitting beside him. Her hand was holding a rifle barrel as if it were an icicle. She looked at me with the same vacant expression she had given me in camp. Something was wrong with her and I decided that she must be abused, badly autistic or cursed with some other disability.

"I'm looking for Jerry, you know him?"

"I'm his father. He's out hunting." He spoke with a hiss and was missing his front teeth.

"You guys get any elk yet?" I asked.

His tongue rolled around his gum line and then he looked down towards my rear tire. "Shit no, it's too goddamned hot."

I didn't like his answer. He'd had to think about it and it wasn't a tough question. When he'd finally chosen his answer, he had to look away. After they drove off, I took a deep breath and thought about the misery my investigation and whatever Claude was up to might dump on this nameless woman's doorstep.

# *Chapter 12*

I spent the evening driving the roads, looking for Dowling and the rest of his crew, and glassing for elk with Nick on the front seat. There'd been three ranch trucks pass me. As they'd approach, I'd put sunglasses on and crunch down my camouflage ball cap. They'd wave by raising their chins. I knew the last driver. His head had rotated and I worried that he'd recognized me.

Other than a handful of jackrabbits and the ranchers, the place was dead. After dark, I returned to my camper and fed Nick. I put my camp chair in the bed of the truck and watched for spotlighters in the distance, chewed on chicken and wondered what I would do if I saw somebody working a light. The white mist of the Milky Way arced across the Pahsimeroi and I saw two shooting stars. It was the same sky the Shoshone Indians had studied for thousands of winters and had given them pause to bless this place with its name. Coyotes yipped and howled up and down the valley as if they owned it. Maybe they did. Sometime after midnight, I crawled into my little camper and went to sleep. It was a remarkable night to be a game warden.

In the morning, I lifted the teardrop's galley lid, made a quick pot of coffee and got out on the county road. After an hour of cruising around like a road hunter and wondering about the lie Claude had told me, I saw Dowling's gold GMC coming. I stopped and waited in the southbound lane until he pulled up. His passenger was the guy with the acne scars, twisted ears and incessant stare.

I got out with the brown paper bag, pulled a six-pack of Budweiser from it and passed it through the window. I was watching Dowling's eyes for anything that told me he was holding a fistful of ugly cards. His pupils were shrunken down to tiny black spots.

"I wanted to give you these," I explained. "Sorry they're not cold."

Dowling's face lit up and his pupils flared. His passenger kept staring at me with his own black-bean eyes, cradling his rifle between his knees.

"Really appreciate your help," I said looking back at Dowling. "I did what you told me and I damned near got one. I was just too slow. There were about a dozen, so thanks."

He flashed his yellow teeth. His eyes glowed their odd green color and got bigger. His right hand rested on a revolver that lay on the seat. "You get some shooting in on the fuckers?"

"Too slow. Maybe tonight." I tilted my head. "Maybe next week."

I got back in my truck and watched through the side mirror as the two drove off. I set my hand on Nick's head. My neck hairs were up–I thought I had caught something in his lizard eyes, some flicker of a ghost, but it could have been my imagination or perhaps a reflection of my own paranoia. Perhaps he had seen something in my eyes that had caused him to pull his cards in tight while gaining some comfort from the cold steel that sat beside him.

If the other man had indeed compromised me, then Dowling was a better poker player than me. But this wasn't a card game, and I had no idea what tremor he'd seen in *my* eyes. Nor did I know how hinked up–suspicious–he was or what hand he thought I might be holding. Whatever nuance I may have imagined, the cold fact was that his right hand had been resting on his revolver. It wasn't what I'd call normal and it bothered me. I had no idea if he had done it subconsciously or whether it was deliberate. Was he trying to send me a message? Did Dowling know who I was? Was he playing out a fantasy in his alcoholic brain?

# Chapter 13

When I got back to Salmon, I stopped at the Regional Office and pulled an inch-high pile out of my mailbox. It was bureaucratic stuff I didn't want to deal with.

I headed home and got on my work computer. I ran the license plate that was on the RV. It was registered to William Molony, age forty-four with a Pocatello address.

Opening up the Fish and Game license database, I found him in the system. It showed his height was 6'6". I was disappointed. I had hoped the man with the crooked ears owned this RV and this plate would unlock his identity.

Molony's license history showed a long string of Middle Fork elk tags. What jumped out though, was his purchase of archery antelope tags for the last two years. Any rifle hunter who had pursued these speed goats in their sagebrush habitat would agree that the ability to make long shots out past 200 yards and farther was a necessity and would have looked crossed-eyed at someone trying to hunt them with a bow.

In reality, I knew several serious archers who harvested pronghorns every year and dedicated a month to the pursuit. They'd put up blinds near water holes and sit for days in the burning sun before taking a shot. Their resolve would have given them considerable deference with the Shoshone who must have used the same technique. But I couldn't believe Molony or his kids were bowhunters.

I was convinced Bill Molony was abetting his sons attempt to kill an antelope with a rifle and cover it with his archery tag. It was one hell of a way to raise his kids—the opposite of what my father had drilled into my brother and me. Dad had more or less raised us in a duck blind and gifted us with the fact that there was no gray in or outside the blind. The laws were to be followed and deviant behavior wasn't on our menu.

Opening up my three-page report, I added two additional pages that described my Molony and Dowling contacts and included the details of giving the beer to Gerald Dowling. I didn't include my fear that Dowling was hinked up or mention the stare from his friend with the crooked ears.

But in thinking about the beer, it got my dander up. You can't buy beer and charge it to the State of Idaho, at least not without going through the chain of command. My boss wasn't going to understand how giving alcohol to the target of a criminal investigation was going to help my cover and make me safer. He'd be concerned that I was throwing cold water on the case. He might have argued with me that I should be giving Dowling a Buck knife or some other hunting gear, but I didn't think he would understand how a six-pack of beer could subconsciously help convince Dowling that I wasn't a cop. It was too out-of-the box for a man who had spent his career in uniform being as truthful as a December day is short. My supervisor had never had to memorize a lie and spin it like the truth to some guy with a hatred for game wardens. And he had never had to do it in a place where a mistake could end in a shallow grave.

It had been grossly easier to spend my own money for the beer and not have to explain something so foreign. My boss would have to read about the beer in my report after the case was ready for prosecution, but for now it would be my secret.

Calling Horsmon, I updated him on my visit to the Pahsimeroi and asked if he had an idea who the person was with the weird ears.

"It almost sounds like a guy who lives here in Challis. He supposedly snagged a salmon off a redd by Warms Springs last year."

Horsmon gave me the guy's name. I didn't recognize it, but I'd been the Challis officer for two and half years when I was a rookie. This news bothered me. When you've worked in a town as a game warden with a thousand people, everyone knows who you are within a few months.

After the call, I ran the weird-ear guy through the license database and studied his details. I concluded it could be him and immediately sent off a photo request to the state police for both he and Molony. I added a lie to the email, stating that there were exigent circumstances and I needed the pictures today.

During the previous year, my boss had pointed out that I was famous for letting my inbox get moldy before I shuffled through the stack of documents that collected in it. I'd promised him I'd step up to the plate, but so far, my efforts had been marginal. I stared at the pile of papers and procrastinated by making a pot of coffee.

Armed with a cup of black brew, I pulled the first memo off the stack. It was a request to help spawn kokanee salmon at a hatchery in north Idaho. I wadded it up and managed to hit my trash bucket. The next memo was from the Regional Supervisor, and addressed the issue that several employees were still violating the department's policy by using their cell phones while driving. It, too, became a round ball and made the bucket.

The third set of papers got my attention. It was a multi-paged memo from the same office supervisor–addressed to my supervisor–with the subject line that read, "Lemhi County Fair and Enforcement Presence."

It started off with a paragraph that explained how the local fair would be beneficial to the department's enforcement mission. I skimmed over the body of the front page and flipped to the next sheet. It was clear that the Regional Supervisor expected every officer to volunteer to sit in the department's booth for a minimum of four hours. The third page had a list of times and dates that needed coverage.

I picked up my cell phone and speed dialed my boss.

I briefed him on the Patterson case: how Horsmon had gotten wind of the camp, what I knew about the players, what had happened to the school, what Dowling had told me, and my suspicions of Molony. I didn't tell him about the beer or my concern that somebody in the camp knew who I was.

His questions and comments showed the support I expected. Then I brought up the county fair. I told him why it would be nuts for me to sit under a Fish and Game banner while hundreds of people strolled by.

"I hear you," he said in an even tone. "But this is coming from the Regional Supervisor. He was clear about it in the staff meeting. He mentioned the director's office was pushing it too."

My supervisor ended the conversation by promising to talk to the RS but wouldn't commit to giving me a pass.

I hadn't had a problem with telling my boss about my local undercover work. If anyone had a need to know, it was him. If the case turned to crap, he would be the one to explain to Boise what had gone wrong. In an effort to get me out of the fair, he'd undoubtedly talk to the Regional Supervisor—who wasn't law enforcement—and he'd want to know the details about the investigation.

The first undercover case I had worked had been four years into my career. It took place in the northern part of the state near Orofino and Lewiston. I had been assigned by Boise and the need-to-know loop had been tightly controlled. The individual who supervised me back then knew I was on special assignment, but hadn't been told where I was working or what I was pursuing. It bugged him. After several weeklong trips, I crossed over to dealing and playing with the crooks. When I returned to Salmon from one of these journeys, my boss pushed for information and I stupidly provided a report that he later admitted showing to another person.

The following week, I was back on a remote forest road above Orofino with the target. He warned me to be careful because he'd heard there was an undercover operation buying fish in the area. My blood turned to ice. The guy was built like a bank safe and hated game wardens. It had been a month since I had purchased a dozen steelhead from him and that was the information my report disclosed to my boss. If this guy had thought about it, he would have killed me in a heartbeat and thrown my corpse in a cedar jungle.

# Chapter 14

I kept checking my email and finally saw the message sitting in my inbox with two attachments.

I clicked on the first JPEG. William Molony's face gawked down as if he was standing on a stump. His hair was shorter and he looked younger than when he'd given me the snake-like handshake. Another mouse click opened the second photo. A male with weird ears and acne pockmarks that looked like nasty burn scars stared at me with a told-you-so look. Horsmon had been close, but this wasn't Dowling's sidekick.

My phone buzzed. It was Mark Armbruster, the other Challis game warden. Mark had schooled me in my rookie years in Challis and had saved my bacon from angry mobs more than once.

"Hey, Horsmon told me to call."

"Probably to tell me how many pounds of bluegill you caught on vacation."

The Pahsimeroi was Armbruster's patrol area and the last thing I needed was for him to bump into me while I was undercover with the Patterson trolls and watch his jaw drop. I really needed to bring him into the loop.

"Horsmon tell you what I've got going?"

"No, he wouldn't say." I could tell he was miffed and I regretted that I hadn't briefed him.

I explained the case from start to finish. It was clear that Armbruster was okay with the fact that I was working it.

"I got a call last night that was like the one Horsmon got," he explained. "Horsmon said to call you—wouldn't say why. Sounded like there was some big secret. Now I get it."

"Is this the same rancher who phoned Horsmon or somebody else?" I asked.

"No, a different guy, different deal. He's afraid of them. Said they've got tattoos and earrings and look scary. Sounds like some scuzz-butts I checked over there last year. Said he was willing to testify at first and then said he wouldn't."

I had never met a rancher who was easily intimidated; this puzzled me, but I saw no reason to ask who his source was.

"What did he see?" I asked trying to get to the point.

"He called them the Patterson group."

I didn't like this answer. It confirmed that the word was out in the Pahsimeroi that we had our eyes on this crew. Sooner or later, somebody would tell Dowling.

"Said he and his kid watched them shoot eleven times from McCoy Lane. Dropped a cow."

The more I thought about a rancher who wasn't willing to testify, the more it pissed me off. I was tempted to ask Armbruster to call the guy back and ask if his kid would be willing to testify.

I took a breath of air. "How many shooters?"

"A bunch. Said he counted nine people and three vehicles. They'd chased the elk through the sagebrush with their rigs. Couldn't see who was doing the shooting with all the dust they were kicking up."

"He get plates?"

"Just the one. It's your guy, Gerald Dowling, Blackfoot. Said one of the other rigs had an Arkansas plate and the other was from Pennsylvania."

I thought about asking him about a guy with weird ears, but let it go.

It was time to hitch up my teardrop.

# *Chapter 15*

A few miles south of Salmon, Deputy Stratton's county truck passed me. Almost immediately, my phone vibrated.

Stratton's voice growled. "I just came from Patterson. Dowling's a dickhead."

I smiled. "How'd you manage to piss him off?"

"Told him about the school and that I was looking for kids driving a white van. Got all wound up. Asked if I had a warrant to be in his camp."

"You pull your gun on him?"

His voice lowered. "Shuddup."

"Were the kids there?"

"The teacher said the van was there this morning. She was cleaning the place up. After Dowling's cheese slid off, I drove up the valley looking for them. They're probably on the other side, hanging in Custer County."

"He say anything about elk?"

"You don't understand; we weren't holding hands and singing Kum Ba Yah. It was close to assholes and elbows."

After the call, I wound along the Salmon River towards the Pahsimeroi and thought about an angle on the school. If his kids had dueled with fire extinguishers, they must have been covered in white powder. Unless Dowling had been too drunk, he would have asked and would have caught the lie. The school had suffered thousands of dollars of damage. If the two kids got tagged for it, he would be the one writing the check. I couldn't see the kids bragging to an older guy like me about destroying the school. And I couldn't see any way to bring it up with Dowling.

I had decided to drive up the valley on the Custer side to avoid going by the camp with my teardrop. No one in the Dowling clan had yet asked where I was staying and I wanted to keep it a mystery. When I got to Ellis, there was a woman walking out of the post office towards a truck who made my jaw drop. It was the same lady who had eyeballed me in the assessor's office when Leroy Barnes name had been mentioned. For a moment, I thought about turning around and getting her plate, but kept on going. Almost everyone that used this post office lived in the Pahsimeroi and I was now convinced she knew Barnes. I wondered how many people–and whom–she had told about my interest in Patterson.

Dark drift smoke from a far-away forest fire was rolling in from the west. It was thick and had turned the sun to marmalade. It made my truck's shadow look blacker as it rolled along the asphalt.

When I came to McCoy Lane, I turned and crossed the Pahsimeroi River. This far up, it was a narrow spring between two bands of willows. The water was clear with bright green patches of watercress and the shade under the brush begged for a hopper fly.

Past the bridge, there were three round alfalfa fields irrigated by wheel lines. The green fields marked the edge of the grey sagebrush plain that went all the way to the Lemhis. A quarter mile from the fields and a hundred yards off the road, six or seven ravens marked what must be the kill site from the shooting Armbruster's witness had described. Tire tracks jolted off the road where the convoy of poachers had chased the elk into the sage. As I drove past the spot, I studied the dusty road surface for brass shells, but none caught my eye.

Once again, I turned off the county road, drove down the two-track and parked the teardrop camper in the tall sagebrush. I had a flat three-gallon jug with a four-inch hole cut in the side. I flipped it over and filled it with water. The hole allowed Nick to drink and as the truck bounced on the rough roads, very little water would spill from it. I filled his food bowl, and parked my camp chair and watched him eat. It was time to get in role and become Pisano. I spoke my undercover name, "Pisano, Tony Pisano," while watching Nick eat. I couldn't help but think of her. She'd been a fish biologist and loved camping in our teardrop. I shook the memory off. It was time to put the past behind me and think of Tony Pisano from Hailey, Idaho, his property management business, and road-hunting elk in the Pahsimeroi.

I uncased my bolt-action .35 Whelen rifle and loaded the staggered magazine with four cartridges, pushed the top round down with my fingertips and closed the bolt on the empty chamber. The rifle had been built on a 98 Mauser action that dated back to the Battle of the Bulge. I'd always wondered about its dark history. I re-cased the gun and slipped it into the cab. My shell box with sixteen brass cartridges was on the dash along with my hunting knife and binoculars. I was wearing an old pair of Levi's, a camouflage shirt and camo ball cap. I walked around the passenger side, and made sure an errant ticket book or some other marker wasn't showing.

I'd bought another six-pack of Budweiser. It was in a small iced cooler on the truck's rear jump seat. I pulled a can out, snapped the top, took a mouthful and let it slide down my throat, while studying the dry Lemhi range to the east. The smoke had stratified but didn't seem to be settling into the valley. I didn't care too much for pale lager beers, but it was cold and tasted good. I dumped the rest of the beer into the grass and refilled the can with water.

I had Nick jump in the back of the truck and thought about eating dinner, but I was too wired. I put Nick's water jug in the bed and closed the tailgate. It was time to go to work.

# *Chapter 16*

When I turned off the pavement towards the camp, a red Dodge four-door pickup with Pennsylvania plates was headed my way. There were four men inside. Both driver-side windows were open and exposed men wearing camouflage and week-long beards. They were holding rifle barrels like broomsticks and staring at me as if something was wrong. I raised my hand off the steering wheel but didn't get a response other than the rattle of the truck's diesel engine as it slid by me.

The camp looked busy. Claude's faded green International Travelall was parked next to Dowling's gold GMC pickup. The black Dodge truck from Arkansas was parked near the cabin. Molony's RV was gone. None of the camp trailers had been moved, and the garbage piles had gotten bigger.

I could see eight people in camp. Most were sitting in camp chairs. All of them had drinks in their hands. I recognized Claude, his wife, and Jerry Dowling. Trixie was sitting with one leg propped on a man's lap that looked like he could be Leroy Barnes. Crooked Ears was missing.

When I opened my door, I stepped out holding the beer can.

Dowling yelled out, "It's my buddy." His voice was slurred and he sounded sincere but his eyes didn't convince me.

As I walked towards him, I heard a boisterous voice to my left, *"First game warden I ever saw walk into a camp with a Budweiser in his hand."*

The air left my lungs and my senses popped. I could hear my heart thumping and my feet flopping in the dust. My eyes looked down a tunnel. The blood in my brain turned to slush. I realized the voice had a hiss and must have come from Claude. I continued walking towards Dowling, feeling like a horse wearing blinders–afraid to look at Claude–while trying to read Dowling's face for some indicator of where this was going. His green eyes glowed with dull amusement and he had a drunken smile.

I was scared shitless.

Dowling motioned towards the cottonwoods with his cigarette. "We got four cooling in the creek."

My gut told me to fold my cards and get the hell out. I kept my eyes on Dowling and listened for another catcall from Claude. What had been his point? Had Crooked Ears burned me? Or had this old ex-con smelled a cop and was fishing for a reaction?

I followed Dowling down a trail into the cottonwood jungle as laughter came from the camp. Claude's voice was still echoing in my brain. I had no idea what his intent had been. It had sounded more like a declaration than a challenge. Whatever he was up to, it was frightening. Claude Dowling knew game wardens worked undercover, and at the very least, I was sure he and his pals had talked about me in that context. They had probably argued whether I was or wasn't. I ran my hand over my pants pocket and made sure I had my keys.

Four unskinned elk carcasses formed a morbid dam in the creek. Water as clear as glass ran over their bodies. They were laid out with their dark heads and manes touching the far bank. Their legs were upstream and their yellow rumps were facing me. Each was tied to a cottonwood tree with a hank of orange baling twine. Each had an elk tag tied to a leg.

Claude's voice was still echoing in my brain but I had to play my hand. I stooped down and stuck my hand in creek. It was cold. I'd never seen carcasses stashed like this.

I could see where small triangular notches had been cut from the tags documenting the supposed kill dates. I turned towards Dowling and looked up at his face. The whites of his eyes were red and glassy and his skin was slick with sweat.

"Never seen this before. They keep okay in the water?"

His face had pinched down and he stood within a boots kick of me. He had a hard smell that hid the fresh scent of the creek.

"Works good. Too fuckin' hot for hanging."

I dipped my hand back in the water. "That's a lot of good meat."

"I shot three of these fuckers the first night I was here." He paused and inhaled from his cigarette. "Leroy and I got up early two days ago and we both got one."

His brag caught me. In court, a boast doesn't mean a lot, but he'd just stepped towards a felony and a stack of misdemeanors. What stopped me, though, was his reason for his boast. Did it mean he trusted me, or was he fishing for my reaction? Or was this his ego lusting for sugar?

I nodded towards McCoy Lane. "Up the valley?"

Dowling's eyes quit smiling and they regained their unblinking lizard look. "Yeah, me and my other buddy come up Friday and that's when I got three." He flicked his cigarette into the creek and it hissed like a bull snake.

His use of "other" seemed to include me. For the moment, I decided to hold my cards and stick around, but my heart was still racing.

"Leroy and I were shooting from six hundred yards. I hit mine on the fourth shot and he got his right after mine dropped." He paused and pointed. "That fucker right there is mine."

"That's some serious shooting," I said.

"My dad got one of 'em."

I recalled Claude's hesitation in his Travelall and where he'd looked when I'd asked him about elk. This confirmed his lie.

"Who got the other one?"

Dowling looked down at the elk. "Shit, who the fuck was it?" He studied the carcasses, frowned and looked confused. "Oh, Jake! It was Jake. The birthday boy."

"That your oldest?"

"No, Jake's from Pennsylvania. You passed 'em on the road. That was my brother Ernie driving."

I was trying hard to keep this story together. I was looking at four elk. Dowling's bouncing story had told of six or seven and he claimed he'd killed four of them. But where were the other two or three, and whose tags were on these four elk?

I looked up at him, still kneeling by the creek. "You guys are gonna run outta bullets."

"Dad didn't even have to shoot. Somebody else hit it."

That confirmed seven elk if I understood his chaotic story.

"Your boys get any shooting in?"

Dowling frowned. "They left an hour ago. Told them to get the hell out of here and stay out of trouble. Little shits were stealing my beer."

We walked back into camp. The sun was behind my back and Claude was squinting up at me. His bald head shined with sweat that ran into his pork chops. His odd young wife was sitting next to him with her bald forehead framed with her long black hair. They made a strange pair.

I took a sip of water from the Budweiser can. "You're Jerry's dad, eh?"

He laughed. "That's what she claimed." His eyes tracked over to an old gray-haired women sitting on the steps of a trailer smoking a cigarette. She wore a long pink bathrobe and fuzzy slippers. She was as white and skinny as a bone and it came to me that she was probably Dowling's mother and Claude's ex. Claude's wife looked down and her blank face managed to frown.

"This is quite the family gathering." I raised the Budweiser like a toast. "I think it's pretty cool. You must be proud to have your sons gathered here, hunting like this." I took another swallow, "You guys leave any for me?"

Claude rolled his tongue across his bare upper gum and studied my face. He fingered his nose with his thumb, stared into my eyes and bobbed his head. "We got seven or

eight of them. Bill and his boys took theirs home already."
He took a drink from his plastic cup. "I didn't even have to
get my rifle out. The goddamn thing was still steaming."
For a moment his eyes jerked back and forth. "All's I had to
do was gut it. There's plenty more up here."

My pulse dropped a notch. It sounded as if he had just
admitted tagging an elk that had been killed by another
shooter. Thus his elk was unlawfully possessed. Perhaps he
*had* been fishing and decided that I hadn't bit his bait.

Dowling put a hand on the man's shoulder sitting with
Trixie. "This is my half-brother, Leroy."

Leroy Barnes was skinny with a hooked nose. His face
was trimmed with a mustache and a soul patch below his
lower lip. His brown hair was long and pulled back into a
ponytail. One ear was pierced and sported a diamond stud.
He wore old jeans, running shoes, and a blue muscle shirt
that was cut low in the armpits and exposed his ribby chest.

I nodded at him. "I'm Tony Pisano. Jerry said you got
yours running at 600 yards. That's a helluva shot. What do
you shoot?"

"Seven mag." His voice was slow and slurred.

"Flat shooter." I said.

Barnes' lips broke into a crooked smile. "I'm gonna try
and smack another one tonight."

Trixie giggled. She still had on the camo halter top and
cut-off jeans. The way she was sitting made her breasts
seem bigger. Her feet were bare and dirty with red painted
nails. Her hair was still greasy.

Dowling pulled an ice pick out of a piece of firewood and smiled at me, flashing his missing tooth. "You huntin' tonight?"

"Absolutely."

He turned, opened a cooler, and attacked a block of ice with the pick. His fingers were wrapped around the wooden handle and had turned white, his face was as red as apple and a vein throbbed near his temple.

As he beat on the block, he spoke in a harsh hammered tone. "Leroy and I are gonna head out soon."

He scooped the ice chips into a plastic guzzler, closed the lid and set it on the cooler. Turning to another cooler, he produced a fifth of Jack Daniel's and topped off the mug. He took a sip, turned to me and frowned. The ice pick was still in his hand and he was tapping it on his leg like a drumstick.

"Wanna go with us?"

# Chapter 17

As I walked towards my truck, I thought about Dowling's invitation. When he'd thrown the offer out, his eyes had gotten serious. The way he'd drummed with the ice pick could have been taken as a threat. Because of this– and Claude's game warden allegation–I wasn't keen on getting in a truck with these guys, especially since Dowling was toast and his half-brother wasn't far behind. With the four dead elk, Dowling's statements, and follow-up interviews, I was somewhat optimistic that we might be able to get a successful prosecution on him for multiple elk. We could probably get Claude to admit–on the record–that somebody else had killed his elk and with luck get the name of the shooter. I assumed that Barnes had used his own tag, and if it was true he was an Arkansas resident, his elk was unlawfully killed and possessed. Logic was telling me to say adiós and get the hell out, but optimism had bit me before. There were too many ifs in my thinking.

A freshly flattened Keystone beer can caught my eye. It was lying in the dirt on the edge of the road. Next to it was a shoe track pushed into the dust. It caused me to pause. The impression consisted of thick zigzagging bars. The breeze had come up and in thirty minutes this print would be in the wind. I took another swallow from the Budweiser can, looked towards the school and bit my lip. It was time for Pisano to join the party.

*****

Dowling's truck was as dusty as a flower sack and smelled of dead mice and stale beer. Crumpled Budweiser cans lay on the floor with a handful of empty cartridge cases and a wadded up fast-food sack.

I set my cased rifle inside.

Barnes and Trixie were snuggled next to each other in the back seat. Both were drinking from plastic cups and laughing at a joke he'd made about a rice-eating Chinese and a black bartender. He'd used the pejoratives, Chink and nigger, all spoken with his rifle set between his knees, barrel-up with the muzzle under his drunken smirk.

Dowling was in the driver's seat and his yellow ball cap was set slightly off-center. His plastic guzzler, topped with whiskey, was in one hand, and he held a cigarette in the other. His rifle was crammed between his left leg and the door, with the muzzle up towards his shoulder. The polished walnut grip of a revolver stuck up between his thigh and console.

It was a poacher's dream.

Dowling looked at me. "Better pull that fucking thing out of its scabbard and get it ready."

I removed my rifle from the case, and set the muzzle on the floor. I nodded. "She's loaded for bear."

Dowling dropped the transmission in gear. "Let's go find those fuckers."

My foot clunked on a beer can. Looking down, I confirmed what I already knew—I was back in the toilet. I'll go to my grave with the thought that hit me as I shut the door: *I'm getting too old for this shit.*

For the last fifteen years of my career, I always had a long-term undercover case I was working. Most of the people I'd worked had been clones of Dowling with big egos and a bizarre urge to break the law. These people would often go out of their way to do it. They would kill a deer, elk or any other living critter as if they were squishing a tick they'd pulled from the nape of their dog. I'd slept in their houses, ate meals with their families, high-fived with them over freshly killed animals and convinced them I was their best friend. After all of that, I'd sworn out search warrants, raided their homes and then testified against them at trial. I was a Judas without any regrets, but I was two years from retirement and ready to get out of the gutter and leave their bullshit behind.

Dowling's drunkenness had left me with an ethical dilemma. My first duty as an Idaho peace officer was for the safety of the public, and I was about to let those people down. The only way I could rationalize allowing him to drive was the lack of traffic in the Pahsimeroi. The other issue was my own safety. I was a fool to have gotten in this truck and a double fool for not putting my seatbelt on. Dowling had a long history of no-belt tickets and I didn't need to glance in the back to see if Barnes and Trixie were wearing theirs. I'd never seen a drunken poacher use a seatbelt; it was part of the culture. If I snapped mine on, it would confirm Claude's theory and might drastically reduce my lifespan. But perhaps they had already decided I was a warden, and this ride wasn't what Dowling had claimed it was.

To top off my stupidity, I hadn't told Horsmon or my boss that I was headed back to the Pahsimeroi. Stratton was the only officer that had an inkling of what I was up to and I hadn't asked him to flight-follow me. Dowling's invitation had caught me one-footed. I was getting paid $23 an hour to ride around with a gunned-up drunk who said I was his buddy when his eyes said otherwise.

# *Chapter 18*

We headed out of the camp, turned south on the county road and drove up the valley.

Dowling pulled his guzzler out of the cup holder and took a drink. "Yesterday, I had my buddy chase them out to us on that ranch down there." He nodded towards the river. "The fuckers were hanging by that rich guy's airstrip. We were too late getting there. Too many fucking people. We should have been there at daybreak. Manuel chased them right to us. They was headed right at us, but these other assholes were down there in their fucking pickups running along the fence. There was like six trucks waiting for them fuckers and they was gonna come out." He set his guzzler into the cup holder and took a deep drag on his cigarette. "My buddy works on that ranch and was chasing 'em for us."

"He on a four-wheeler?"

Dowling nodded. "Yeah, he works for the guy that owns the ranch. But what the asshole doesn't know is that he's my buddy. He's a good Mexican." Dowling turned to me with a shit-eating grin. "He's Mexican but he's a good guy."

I knew who Manuel was. He'd been involved in another case that I had investigated overtly and he was well aware of what I did for a living. Chasing elk for hunters with a motorized vehicle was another rock in the box, but unless Manuel admitted it, it wasn't going to get prosecuted, since none of these people were going to testify against anybody. What pissed me off was that we'd had two witnesses report the Patterson group's shenanigans, so why hadn't someone reported these other road-hunting assholes, as Dowling had labeled them? My guess was that the other so-called hunters were locals from Challis. Locals protected locals, but hated flatlanders from southern Idaho who were killing "their" elk.

As we continued up the road, we passed alfalfa fields on the left and a sagebrush flat on the right that stretched all the way to the cottonwoods along the river. Dowling and Barnes chattered about bear baits they had placed in the upper valley and whether or not they should check to see if they'd been hit. I knew from their license history printouts that neither had purchased the necessary bait permits.

At the Big Creek bridge, we crossed the county line. I could see the red Dodge from Pennsylvania sitting off to the side of the road.

Dowling squinted his eyes. "This is where I killed ten of the fuckers last year."

He'd said the word "fuckers" like it was a piece of gristle that he'd spat out.

As he pulled up to the Dodge, I tried to catch the plate but failed. There were four aboard and I could see three rifle barrels sticking up. I scanned the passengers looking for Crooked Ears, but couldn't tell if he was on the far side. Dowling got out and talked with the driver while I engaged Barnes about the regulations.

"I'm confused about this cultivated field deal."

"You have to be within a mile of one of these fields but most of the time—as long as you're in the valley—you're within a mile."

I marveled at this claim. Half or more of the valley consisted of sagebrush plains or rolling hills that were miles from a cultivated field.

Dowling got back in the truck and smiled at me. "Ernie's wondering who you are."

"I'm wondering who the hell Ernie is and all those guys he's got with him."

Dowling flipped his cigarette out the window. "He's my brother and that's his buddies from back east."

"Easterners are different," I frowned and looked at him, "and loose lips sink ships."

We turned off the pavement onto a two-track road that wandered through the sagebrush towards a low ridge. An alfalfa field was about a half-mile behind us.

Dowling motioned towards the top of the hill where we were headed. "This hilltop is the legal limit. Beyond that, we need to make sure nobody's watching. It's where I got into 'em the first night I was here."

"Last year?"

"This year."

Claude's Travelall was parked near the crest and it appeared that he was watching the field to the north. His wife was sitting next to him and I assumed he was going to try to kill an elk that he would launder with her tag. Dowling waved at them as he passed and we continued bouncing into the sagebrush hills to the south.

After about a mile, Barnes put his hand on the front seat and leaned forward. "How many tags we got in the truck, Jerry?"

"I've got one, Tony's got one."

That told me that Barnes had used his tag on the elk he'd killed two mornings ago, and that Dowling must have used somebody else's tags on all of the elk he'd killed. Or he had someone else's tag in his jockey box. The plot was thickening.

Barnes pointed across the dash. "There's a fuckin' herd of them right there!"

I looked but couldn't see any elk. Dowling sped up.

I turned to Dowling. "With us three tonight, how many tags if we get into them?"

"Probably ten." Dowling snorted. "Ernie's got a bunch and dad's wife's got one. But let's worry about that shit when the fuckers are down and kicking. We got plenty of tags."

# *Chapter 19*

Looking in the direction where Barnes had pointed, I wasn't convinced he'd seen elk. They could have topped the spur ridge and disappeared, but I wasn't going to challenge his vision.

"Jesus, Leroy," I said, "you've got eyes for elk!"

Dowling had picked up the pace along the rolling ridge and we bounced over the rocks while he and Barnes discussed which gulley the elk might have disappeared into. We continued moving along the rolling ridge. Both of them were using the F-bomb for elk. The conversation dropped off and for maybe ten minutes we drove in silence, looking for the elk herd. The hill spurred off to a point and we stopped for a pee break. I glanced back at Trixie. She was down on the seat looking like she'd passed out.

"She alright, Leroy?"

"Can't hold her booze."

The view was spectacular and I was willing to bet there weren't any other humans in this immense piece of heaven. Dowling and I stood shoulder-to-shoulder and peed, looking across a ten-mile sagebrush plain. It was as flat as a floor and butted into Mount Borah and the fence-like ridge of the Big Lost Range. Borah pushes through 12,000' and is encircled by limestone peaks named Leatherman, Mountaineer, White Cap, Morrison, Bad Rock, Corruption, and Sacajawea to name a few.

Halfway across the gray plain, the Pahsimeroi River feeds a thin green line of willows and cottonwoods.

That narrow strip of riparian vegetation caused me to stop and think about what was happening. The phrase *The Thin Green Line*, is the symbol of conservation enforcement around the world. That skinny line represents the enforcement effort to keep thieves like Dowling from victimizing wildlife. Critters on one side, crooks on the other, officers in between.

Studying the line of vegetation, while thinking about what I was doing, it struck me that the line was chaotic and broken but none the less, it was there. It reminded me of what my first boss, Al Nicholson, had told me about chasing poachers, "All we can do is try to keep the pot from boiling over."

There I was, an Idaho game warden, marveling at this wild country while peeing with a poacher who couldn't stop bragging about his dirty deeds. A person who had no reverence or respect for the land or its four-legged residents. A person that would sooner or later figure out who he'd peed with. I hoped his revelation would be on my schedule and not his.

Off to the south, the Donkey Hills rose up. It isn't a group of hills. The place is a rolling mountain built with knolls, intersecting ridges and buttes. It's covered with sagebrush and spiked with a few stands of dark timber that's a perfect place for elk to hide. It's an important place to me, since it was where I'd first gazed into the Pahsimeroi. I'd worked as a wildland firefighter in my college days and we had gotten the call right at dark while stationed in the desert south of Arco. I remember driving up the Little Lost River watching the flames light up the

Donkies. We'd worked the fire all night and at first light we built a campfire to warm our C-ration cans for breakfast. We sat and watched the sun top the Lemhi Range to our right and paint Mount Borah's summit in a liquid golden glow that worked down its flank until it covered the valley with warmth. It was like sitting in the balcony of a theatre, watching the beginning of a grand production. In fifteen years of firefighting, it'd been the only fire I worked that had been started by a meteorite. That fact seemed to validate the Pahsimeroi's magic like King Author finding a mythical sword stuck in a boulder. It was a story I wasn't going to share with Dowling and Barnes.

"This is where I was shooting the other day." Dowling shook himself and buttoned his fly. "Clear down to that flat."

"Jesus, how far is that?"

"Eleven hundred yards. I fired from right here and knocked her down. Then she got up running. Those are my tracks straight across that fucking desert."

I could see a set of vehicle tracks that cut a line through the sagebrush so straight it could only have been done at a high rate of speed. Thinking of where we were, we had to be over three miles from the nearest cultivated field.

"That's where I shot that last cow up. Those are my tracks. I chased that motherfucker at seventy and eighty miles an hour. I came off this hill and shot straight across that fucking flat."

His story bothered me. This place was like Idaho's own Valley of the Gods. Dowling had defiled it.

We got back in the truck and I glanced at Trixie. She was squinting like she had a headache and she scowled at me.

"How many elk were in that bunch?" I asked.

Dowling finished his whiskey. "About thirty. The fucker finally quit in that green brush out along the creek and then I shot her in the head."

"This's from a couple of mornings ago?"

"No, this was my first night here. Me and my buddy Bill and his kids." His eyes got wide, took on their glassy lizard look and he stared at me. "What do you do for a living?"

My hackles came up. His slurred speech was gone. It sounded like he'd managed to sober up despite his continued drinking. I'd asked one too many questions.

"Property management. I rent houses to rich assholes."

For a second, he continued to look at me like he was reading a book and then his eyes pinched down. He reached for the ignition and started the truck.

It was my turn. "How do *you* make a buck?"

"I'm a roofing contractor."

"I need to get your business card."

# Chapter 20

We continued off the point and into the flat. I wondered if Dowling's wife's tag was in the jockey box or if he'd used it to launder one of the elk in the creek.

"Your wife come up and camp with you and the kids?"

He acted like he hadn't heard me. After a full minute, he pulled a cigarette out of a pack of Camels that had been sliding on the dash. He lit it with a deep inhale and let the smoke roll out of his nose.

"Not anymore."

"Divorce, eh?"

He looked at me but his eyes were focused across the valley. "Found her hanging in the garage."

I took a deep breath. "Jesus Christ, Jerry, you've gotta be shitting me."

It had come out of nowhere and hit me like a baseball bat. It put me back to my wife's bedside, while holding her hand and watching her slip.

I looked at him and bit my lip. "God." I had an unbearable urge to tell him *my* story but held it back. "When the hell was this?"

"About a year ago."

We were both traveling the same greasy road of grief, but I could not bring my Jan into this truck. I looked at my ring finger where my wedding band had been and rubbed it with my thumb. The indentation and stencil of untanned skin were gone. I'd taken the ring off after meeting a widow in Bozeman who had travelled this same slippery road. She had been helping me through the worst times of my life.

It's been my experience that grief is seasoned with guilt and regret, and Dowling's must have been over-cooked and hard to chew. I was sure the alcohol hadn't softened it. For a half mile we bounced over a rocky two-track in silence and I wished I'd brought a cold beer. The road ended at a spring that tied into the Pahsimeroi. Two magpies and a raven flew out of a patch of green greasewood and changed the mood.

"That's where the fucker died."

"You have some help loading it, I hope?"

"My buddy Bill was with me."

"This is the one you shot from way back on the hill?"

He stopped the truck, stuck his arm out the window and pointed back to the point of the ridge. "I hit her right in the fucking ass from up there. She ran this fucking far." He pointed toward the greasewood. "You can see my tracks going in the brush."

He dropped the transmission in gear and turned around. I realized that he'd brought me here to tell his poaching story and shovel coal into his ego's boiler. I looked to the east and guessed we were pushing four miles from a cultivated field.

We followed the feeder coming from the spring, mudded through it and angled across the flat towards the Pahsimeroi.

Barnes reached across the seat and pointed beyond the windshield. "There's an antelope way out there."

It was a lone buck with a heavy black cheek patch and skinny horns.

Barnes' speech had gotten slower and his southern accent was deeper. "I'll tell you right now, I ain't using that antelope tag unless it's safe."

Dowling snorted. "We want a big buck anyway."

I was sure they were talking about using Bill Molony's tag and wondered how they'd try to pass off a carcass with an exit wound the size of a fist as an archery kill.

This far up the valley, the Pahsimeroi River was an intermittent stream that had cut itself down into a gulley and was locally called the dry beds. Dowling dropped the gearbox into low. We four-wheeled through a few inches of water and climbed back up to the flat where he found a two-track that cut to the right and we paralleled downstream along the gulley that was marked by scattered cottonwoods. It was the green line I'd seen from the ridge.

It took us an hour to get to Patterson and I don't think five words were spoken. When we pulled into camp, a girl who looked to be fourteen was standing next to my truck and petting Nick.

Trixie stuck her head out the door. "Get away from him. He's psycho!"

I held back a smile.

Dowling put the truck in park and turned to me. "Be here at six-thirty and we'll try it again."

# Chapter 21

When Nick and I got back to our camp, it was dark. Other than the scratching of a cricket, it was quiet. I pulled out a flashlight and studied the dust around the trailer. Dowling had never asked where I was camped and it was bothering me. It didn't make sense unless he already knew the answer. If he was hinked up—and I was convinced he was—he could have sent one of his minions to creep my teardrop while he had me in his truck.

Not finding any red flags, I fed Nick, pulled the cooler out, sat down in my chair and popped open a Budweiser. For two and half hours, I'd felt like I'd been standing on a razor's edge and I was exhausted. I sat sipping on the beer, letting my night vision come back. I thought about Dowling and the grief that had clouded his eyes. I needed to make notes, but I had to unravel before I could sort it out. I pulled a piece of chicken out of the cooler and studied the blackness.

The Milky Way was back and ran across the night sky like a drop of cream in a cup of black coffee. The thin edge of a crescent moon was up and its dark side plugged a hole that looked like one of Dowling's eyes. When I'd first met him, his eyes didn't look right. I'd finally written it off as a product of opiates or amphetamines. One moment his pupils would be shrunken points and then his mood would shift and they'd flare as big as a black dime, resembling the eyes of a lizard I'd once seen in the crack of a rock.

Claude's game-warden challenge—or whatever it had been—rang in my ears. I replayed it and once again felt my skin crawl. I watched Dowling's ugly face as he tapped the ice pick and threw out his offer. And again, I studied his lingering expression when I had lied and told him what I— or Pisano—did for a living.

Beyond those misgivings was the one moment that I believed I had gained Dowling's confidence. It had been when he'd shared something from his soul—his confessional about his wife's death. It had grabbed me and if he weren't such an elk-thieving miscreant, it would have been easy for me to hitch my camper and leave his sorry-ass behind.

Dowling's elk-killing stories had been a drunken ramble that I'd tried hard to untangle. He'd told me three different times that on his first night—Friday—he had killed three elk with someone named Bill and he had shown me where one of them had died. He'd reinforced the story by telling me that Bill had helped him load it.

Claude had said that Bill had "taken theirs home," and I assumed they were both talking about Bill Molony, the guy I had met in the RV.

Twice, Dowling had told me that "two days ago"— Sunday—he and his half-brother had each killed an elk. Barnes had bragged about it too, so it was believable. Plus that was the same day that Armbruster's spineless rancher had seen the shooting on McCoy Lane.

Somehow I was under the impression that the elk Claude had tagged had been killed yesterday, and that may have been when Pennsylvania Jake had killed his.

All of this left three missing elk and I assumed that Molony was indeed the "Bill" in this tale and had taken them to Pocatello.

Part of this confusion could be cleared up by sending Horsmon into the camp under the guise of a routine check to obtain the names and kill dates from the tags on the elk in the creek. But it was an hour's drive to cell service and I needed to crank out a pile of notes and get some sleep. Backup would have to wait.

# *Chapter 22*

When I got to Dowling's camp, the sky above the Lemhis was beginning to wake, but first light was still thirty-minutes off. The Milky Way had melted into the twilight but a handful of stars still dimpled what was left of the darkness across the valley. A Coleman lantern lit up the inside of the little cabin. The red dot of a lit cigarette marked someone inside a nearby blacked-out trailer and I had a sense that they were watching me. Other than that, the camp was dead.

I stepped out of my truck with a cup of fresh-brewed coffee. I stood and looked at the camp. The air had puddled in the valley and I tightened my jacket's zipper. A wisp of smoke rose from the fire pit and a dozen or so crumpled and burnt beer cans lay in it. A trace of sewage tainted the air. A raccoon or some other critter had drug a bag of garbage a few feet and scattered empty cans of stew and beans. From the bed of the truck, Nick gazed down the creek, listening to a coyote howl. Ernie Dowling's red Dodge was gone.

The light went out in the cabin. Barnes stepped out and nodded at me. He walked over to the camp trailer with the cigarette glow, hit his fist on the door and yelled, "Git your ass up!" Retrieving his rifle from his black Dodge, he stuck it in the back seat of Dowling's gold GMC. Grabbing my rifle, I met him at the truck and told him he could have the front.

His eyes were red and his hair was loose. He was trying to secure it in a ponytail. "Go ahead. I might need to take a nap."

"Thanks. You live in Blackfoot too?"

"Arkansas."

"Shit, that's a drive. What do you do for a living'?"

"Truck bass boats all over the Gulf Coast."

"Been there long?"

"Half my life."

That admission was a rock in the box, and it meant that any elk with his resident tag was getting seized unless it slipped into the wind.

"When you gotta be back?

"Two weeks."

Dowling came out of the darkened trailer with his rifle slung on his shoulder. He held the mug he'd had the night before. He wore the same dirty jeans, ragged T-shirt and yellow ball cap. Pulling open the driver's door, he scowled at me. "There's some fuckin' aspirin in the jockey box."

I popped it open, found the bottle and handed it to him. "You ain't any prettier in the morning, Jerry."

He smiled and let out a hoarse laugh and washed down the aspirin with whatever was in his cup. The dome light illuminated his greasy face. I caught the skunky odor of marijuana smoke and glanced at his eyes. His pupils were as big as buttons, too big for THC.

Dowling jammed his rifle between the door and his knee and lit a cigarette. After a long drag he reached under the seat, found his revolver, and wedged it next to him. We headed down the valley towards Ellis. After about five miles we turned onto Furey Lane, cut between irrigated fields and crossed the Pahsimeroi. We were on the hunt, Dowling had slowed and it was obvious they expected to see elk. First light was hitting the Big Lost Range but the shadow of the Lemhis still blanketed the valley floor.

Barnes leaned forward. "I think it was right here I shot those two bucks with one shot last year."

"Luck makes meat," I said.

"It weren't luck," Barnes replied, "I could see the bigger one was gonna walk in front of the other one. It was like swatting flies."

Dowling took a drink from his cup. "If you're so fucking lucky, that rancher woulda been in bed and we wouldn't have wasted our tags on the fuckers."

The two half-brothers seemed at ease with me. When I had handed the aspirin to Dowling, his smile had looked sincere. There was no doubt he had initially thought I might be a game warden. This had come to a head when he'd sobered up and asked me what I did for a living. I felt that for now, he'd put it to bed. He enjoyed telling me about his elk killing—it was the numbers thing again—how far he shot, how fast he chased them, and how many he killed. I think he looked upon this killing as the one thing he was successful at. Telling me about it filled his belly. I also believed my elk tag was a potential tool for his hunger. I had no doubt, given the opportunity, he'd try very hard to dump an elk before I could get a shot off. It was all this that had gotten me, or Tony Pisano, into his truck. If we got into elk, I was going to let him feed.

On every undercover investigation I had worked, I had seen this switch from uncertainty to trust and that's when I believed the ice became as thin as glass. These people would start out being paranoid and keep their secrets tight. It was at this point that I believed if they decided I was a warden most would just let it ride and walk away. But after I had convinced them I was their friend, and they spilled their criminal guts, and then found out I was a warden– that's when the ice would crack and I'd tumble into the cold black water.

Dowling had been different than the rest. From the moment I had met him, he had bragged about his crimes even though he had his doubts. It was as if his ego's valve was stuck open and he couldn't shut up. But it wasn't until he'd told me about his wife and now with this hangover-induced mood that I felt like he might be starting to trust me. The ice was thinning and it was time to check my fears and keep my head in the game.

I wished I had made a thermos of coffee. I had never considered myself a morning person. I felt foggy and dull. It worried me. These two seemed to be at ease but, I had no room for error. There were twenty-five questions bouncing in my head, but I had to keep my mouth shut and wait for the right moment.

We turned up the valley on the Custer County Road. After a few minutes, Barnes leaned forward and pointed out a herd of about thirty elk on the far side of an alfalfa field several hundred yards away.

Dowling stopped and studied the hills to the west. "We gotta make damn sure the fuckin' wardens aren't around."

I looked across the same foothills hoping that
Armbruster and Horsmon were still in bed and things
would play out. This was the utmost irony. Dowling and I
wanted the same thing, but for grossly different reasons.

For twenty minutes we sat and watched. It was apparent
that Dowling's plan was to wait for them to leave the field
and then we'd chase and shoot. The elk were nervous. Two
cows and a calf started to leave and then went back the
herd.

Dowling turned to Barnes. "I don't think these fuckers
are gonna leave the field."

It was at this point that I noticed that when Dowling
looked at the elk, his tongue would dart out and run along
his lower lip as if there was a flake of tobacco left from his
cigarette.

From the back seat, Barnes said, "Let's get your buddy
to run the motherfuckers out."

Dowling didn't reply. I found it curious that these guys
would chase elk, kill them far from legal ground, transfer
tags and god knows what else, but they had a fear of
trespassing.

The morning light was settling into the valley and it lit
up a dust plume approaching from behind us. I pointed it
out.

Dowling studied the dust for a moment in his mirror,
dropped the truck in gear and glanced at the elk. "Let's get
the fuck out of here and go work the dry bed." Again, his
tongue touched his lip.

It was chilly out and the windows were up. Dowling lit a
Camel and let the smoke fill the cab. Both half-brothers

were sullen from hangovers and whatever else they'd partied with. Talk was scarce and the party-like mood from the night before had disappeared. We drove past the Pines and turned onto McCoy Lane, crossed the Pahsimeroi and turned up the same road we had come down the night before.

Dowling kept looking in his mirror, then slowed down and stopped. "I think that's Ernie behind us."

The red Dodge pulled in behind and stopped. I turned around and saw Ernie walking towards us. I wasn't sure, but it looked like Crooked Ears was in the passenger seat.

Ernie stuck his head in the window and eyed me. "Why'd you guys take off? There was elk right there."

Dowling flicked his cigarette out the window. "Thought you were the fucking fish cop." His hand went to the grip of his pistol.

"They weren't gonna leave the field anyway," Barnes said. "No sense hanging around."

Ernie was looking towards me, but his eyes were moving right and left like he was thinking. "Some of these guys still want to kill their own elk. That could be a problem." His eyes met mine and he stopped talking. His face was a foot from Dowling's, but he seemed to be trying to figure me out.

It was time for Pisano to step up to the plate. I nodded and spat, "They need to shit or get off the pot."

Ernie looked at Dowling. "What ya wanna do?"

Barnes, Dowling and Ernie kicked around their thoughts like boys playing marbles. It was finally decided that we would drive up the ridge to the east where we'd been the night before and Ernie would work up the bottom along the dry bed.

Dowling bummed two Budweisers from Ernie and we turned around and hit McCoy Lane. I watched as his red Dodge eased along the dry bed.

Out in front of us, I could see a white Ford pickup headed towards us. As it approached, it slowed and I saw the driver was wearing a black cowboy hat. He had a lean jaw and a tanned face. I scrunched my ball cap down. It was Jim Martiny, the local brand inspector and I knew him well. As he passed, he glanced at us and lifted two fingers off the steering wheel.

Dowling watched in the mirror. "I think that's the fucker that made sure we tagged those bucks last year."

I turned around and looked. Martiny had his brake lights on. *Goddamnit*, I thought. "He's stopping for some reason."

Dowling chuffed like a bear and got into the throttle. "We ain't gonna bullshit with his fuckin' ass today."

The taillights went out and I took a breath of air.

# Chapter 23

Dowling seemed to be waking up. I suspected whatever had been in his cup wasn't coffee, and now he was into the beer. We turned onto the ridge road and followed the same path from the night before. We bounced from rock to rock, and I thought about how to lead Dowling into talking about the night he'd killed the three elk.

"When you got that one you had to chase off the point, were the buggers down there in the wash where Ernie's at, or were they up here?"

Dowling had lit another cigarette. "They was up ahead. Other side of that ridge." He pointed to the southwest. "I'll show you when we get over there."

"Was that just a couple of days ago?"

"Friday night."

"You guys been doing some shooting, that's for sure."

"Seven elk." Dowling said. "I shot these three fuckers Friday night." He glanced back at Barnes while his tongue rubbed his lip, "And then those two elk you and I got the other morning, and the one Sam ass-ended, but I don't think it was Sam."

Barnes put his hand on the top of the front seat. "That was an ought-six bullet I dug out of Sam's."

The way he'd said it, sounded as if he agreed that Sam—who ever he was—hadn't hit it.

I counted six elk. Dowling was talking about seven and now I had another name.

I turned back towards Barnes. "Is this where you got yours?"

"No. Me and Jerry shot two more the other morning over there." He pointed towards McCoy Lane. "We had to tag them. We were where everybody could see we had elk down and Jake got another one."

If I'd heard him right, that put Jake's kill on Sunday with Barnes' and Dowling's, but it was confusing. I couldn't figure out a way to edge the question in.

I pulled a fistful of shells out of my shirt pocket, looked at them and turned to Dowling. "Is Ernie gonna be pissed if we lay a pile of them down this morning?"

"We're on Blackfoot time. Ernie'll get his buddies to pony up their fucking tags."

I looked down along the line of cottonwoods and could see Ernie's truck easing along the dry bed. My eyes worked up the drainage, studying the shadows. I had mixed feelings about spotting elk. At the moment, everybody in this party was hunting elk illegally since we were so far from a cultivated field. Anything killed would be flagrantly illegal. I had thought that perhaps Ernie's friends were law-abiding when he said they wanted to shoot their own elk, but I decided I was wrong. They too had to know they were pushing two miles from a field.

We crested the spur ridge and Dowling pointed into a small basin that faced Borah. "Right down there. That's where I laid those two fuckers down that first night with Bill and Sam."

I could see a handful of magpies clustered near something on the ground. The nearest cultivated field was

well over two miles to the east. By now it sounded like
Dowling hadn't used his tag until he killed his fourth elk on
Sunday. I also suspected his tag was on one of the elk that
was lying in the creek. But who was this Sam guy? Bill
Molony had said his sons were in camp antelope hunting.
Dowling had said something about Bill's son.

"Is Bill that great big bastard that I talked to in an RV in
your camp the other day?"

"Yeah, Big Bill Baloney."

"Baloney? For real?"

Dowling laughed. "No, it's Molony, he's so full of
bullshit we call him Baloney."

It's rare for someone to try and move an elk during an
open season without finding somebody who is willing to
(illegally) provide a tag. Usually the crook had one lined up
before he dropped the hammer. Running an untagged elk
happens, but usually at night. Dowling and Barnes had both
cussed about having to tag deer last year and elk this year.
But was it because someone had seen them do the shooting
and they preferred to figure out who was going to tag it
when they were back in camp? Or were they actually brazen
enough to stash untagged elk in their camp? The big
question though, was who, if anyone, tagged the three elk
killed on Friday that Molony had apparently taken home?

# *Chapter 24*

By 11:00, we were back in camp. Ernie pulled in and his crew got out. Crooked Ears wasn't with him.

The only elk we'd seen had been the ones in the field at the Pines. Ernie, Dowling and Barnes had a powwow for an evening hunt. They talked about having Manuel run the elk out of the field, but were concerned about witnesses. Barnes suggested that he could drive his ATV down along Big Creek to flush elk out while Dowling and Ernie paralleled it in their trucks.

Trixie was sitting in a chair rubbing lotion on her tan arms and staring at me. She'd cleaned herself up and was wearing a skimpier top and shorter shorts. Her skin looked fresh. She smiled and asked me if I was ready for a drink. I passed.

I greeted Nick, slipped my rifle back into my truck and made a decision about my next step. One of the hardest decisions to make in an undercover investigation is when to pull the plug. I had uncovered what I believed were six illegal elk. Barnes' kill would be easy because of his residency, but required more work. Claude's elk would take a confession that would somehow need to be corroborated. The three elk that Dowling had claimed to have killed were all well outside the one-mile limit. If he had indeed shot at least one of them, then the elk that he had killed with Barnes two days later was illegal, since it was an over-limit. But the problem with what had happened that day was that the truth was hard to find; Dowling was a serial bullshitter.

Barnes had mentioned recovering a bullet from the elk that Sam had claimed. He'd said it was a .30-'06 bullet. Dowling's rifle, although chambered for a different cartridge, was the same caliber. The way Barnes's had said it told me that even he doubted that Sam had killed that elk. The battle on this investigation was going to be untangling Dowling's twisted tale of what happened on black Friday.

If I kept working this beast–and with luck–I could probably pull Ernie into it along with some of his pals, especially with this afternoon's plan of Barnes using an ATV to bust elk out of Big Creek, which on its face was illegal. The dilemma was that I was here to protect elk, not to watch them pile up like a rick of logs. How many elk needed to die before I shut this killing down?

And what would happen if I ran out of luck? That was the question that had been chewing on me for two days. This was my backyard. I had no business doing this case in a place I had worked as a uniformed officer. I still hadn't figured out who Crooked Ears was and he had seemed to have evaporated. We could easily run into a rancher out somewhere in the hills that might recognized me. He could easily ask Dowling, behind a tailgate, why he was hunting with a game warden. Or the brand inspector could drive into the camp and ask if the warden was still around. There were too many possibilities running through my brain.

I grabbed three Budweisers out of my cooler and pulled Dowling away from his bullshit session he had going with his brothers.

"Hey, these are for you." I handed him the beers and pulled Tony Pisano's elk tag out of my pocket. "I don't think

I'm coming back. I got shit I gotta get done." I'd finally told him the truth. "Is there anyway you could fill my tag? I'll split the meat with you. I can run down to Blackfoot or pick it up here. It ain't that far. I got tax issues."

Dowling's green eyes smiled. "We can fill it for you." He nodded and his pupils got as big as peas. "Try our damnedest."

I handed him my tag and my undercover business card. "Give me your phone number. I'll keep in touch."

Dowling pulled a single cigarette from a pack of Camel's and I dug a pen out of my truck and he wrote his number down on the wrapper and gave it to me.

I handed him a ten-dollar bill. "Gas money. Thanks for the hunt, mi amigo."

Reaching my hand out, he gave me a semi-hug. We shook hands, parted ways, and Nick and I got the hell out of Appalachia.

# Chapter 25

It would take time to conclude this investigation, and in the meantime, this crew was going to be trying like hell to poach more elk. I'd given Dowling my tag as an insurance policy in the event that if either he or his half brother killed another elk, there was a good chance they'd attempt to launder it by using my tag, and that would bite them.

I got back to my camp, grabbed my box of greasy chicken, hitched my teardrop up and headed for Challis. I was doing sixty and my mind was racing. When I came out of the canyon in Round Valley, I called Horsmon. I told him I was ten minutes out and that I needed help.

Horsmon met me in front of his garage, wearing his uniform and gun belt. He was stout like a bear with a neatly trimmed black beard, but looked too young for his receding hairline.

I gave him the short version. He changed into his civvies and we jumped in his personal semi-ancient Tundra pickup and we headed for the Pahsimeroi. Along the Salmon River, I gave him the long version.

We turned just before Ellis and went up the Custer County Road. I figured we had three hours to get the job done before the Patterson crew came out of the camp looking like extras from *The Walking Dead*. The last thing I wanted to do was give them a reason to think something was afoot.

We crossed over McCoy Lane and I pointed out the ravens in the sagebrush. We talked about stopping and getting a DNA sample, but decided to pass since we would be too exposed. The kill site was within one mile of a field, and thus the value of the evidence wasn't worth being seen.

We turned off the lane onto the two-track and bounced for twelve miles along the dry bed until we found the first gut pile that Dowling had shown me the night before.

There were still magpies and ravens working it, but they would starve to death with what was left. The dirt was stained black with blood. Dried green stomach contents from the cow's last meal were scattered around. An empty Budweiser can sat off to the side along with a Camel cigarette butt.

I wasn't optimistic. The sun had baked this scene for five days while the coyotes and corvids had picked it clean and bacteria was feeding on the stain.

I tried to find a piece of gut without any luck, so I collected chunks of bloody soil and crossed my fingers. Red blood cells do not contain DNA. White blood cells do, but comprise only about 1% of the cells in the blood of a healthy animal. Horsmon took photographs and collected the beer can and cigarette butt. I took a GPS reading and we headed for the point where Dowling had said he'd shot from.

Horsmon poked around and located a spent .300 Winchester Magnum casing. We high-fived. I stood and videotaped Dowling's vehicle tracks in the flat below us. We took a GPS reading and drove another quarter mile along the ridge.

Ravens showed us the spot where Dowling had said he killed his first two elk on Friday. Another Budweiser can and Camel cigarette butt confirmed we were in the right spot. Both elk stomachs were intact and were about thirty yards apart. One was too small for an adult cow—it had to be from a calf. We photographed the two scenes, collected the evidence and marked another GPS waypoint. Looking around, I decided the shooting had to have taken place somewhere on the ridge above the gut piles. Horsmon and I looked for brass but after fifteen minutes we hadn't found any. We were running out of time and needed to get off the ridge.

In piecing together Dowling's story—and knowing where all three elk had been killed—it looked like Dowling, Molony, and Sam, must have spotted the elk from the ridge, opened up into the herd from several hundred yards and knocked two down. They then raced behind the herd for about a quarter of a mile to the point of the hill. From there, Dowling had gotten out and flock-shot and crippled the cow. Then they drove off the hill onto the flat and chased her for a mile before she gave up and he shot her in the head. It was a horrific thing to brag about and it made me wonder what dirty tricks Dowling had done to his wife.

# *Chapter 26*

On the way back to Challis, Horsmon and I made plans. He concurred that the elk in the creek needed to be checked in a fashion that wouldn't make the camp suspicious. He also came up with a ruse to get DNA samples.

When we got to his house, I jumped in my truck and Nick and I headed north to Salmon. For fifty-nine miles I thought of Dowling, Barnes, Claude, Crooked Ears and Molony and how that cow elk had been wounded and run until it was at the end of its rope. I thought about Claude's odd wife and the life she'd been dealt. I wondered if the old woman in the pink robe was Claude's ex-wife, and if so, what possessed her to hang in the same camp with the man who must have brought her so much misery. I'd driven between Challis and Salmon a hundred times. This was the only trip I'd made twisting beside the Salmon River without noticing its green turbulent waters and the black cliffs of volcanic rock that framed its canyon.

When I hit cell service, I called Marc Arms, the Regional Investigator in Pocatello. I told him the short version, and asked him to do some digging on Bill Molony and the Dowlings.

My phone had a message from my boss.

"Hey Latham, give me a call when you can. It's about the fair."

I was tempted to throw my phone out the window, but I took a deep breath and called him back.

"You're off the hook. Lukens bought off on your lame excuse after I promised to cover for you in the booth. You owe me."

I pulled over, hoping he didn't catch on to the fact I was driving while using my cell phone. I told him the long version of what had happened in the last two days and where I wanted to go with it. His reaction was nothing short of enthusiastic.

"I assume Horsmon was keeping track of you while you were playing with those shitbags."

I looked at Nick's head that was resting on the console. "Horsmon started this case and I've been keeping him in the loop." For a second I thought about my answer—I didn't want to lie to somebody I respected. "It'd be stupid not to have somebody flight-following me."

When I got home, I fed Nick, ate my last piece of chicken and crawled in the shower. I had found that after a charade with people like Dowling, I always felt as if I had been sitting in front of a smoky campfire fueled by logs of bullshit. Nothing worked better to flush their crap than a long hot shower in the sanctuary of my own home.

My plan for the evening was to crank out notes from the morning hunt, but instead I laid down on my bed and called my lady friend in Bozeman. She told me about a mountain bike ride she'd done with her dogs and I told her how nice my teardrop camping trip with Nick had been. I described the magic of the Pahsimeroi. Ten minutes later I was asleep.

# Chapter 27

An investigation is no better than the paper it's written on. I should have scribbled case notes as soon as I was home, but it didn't happen. With a fresh pot of coffee, I sat down in front of my computer and started typing.

I was just finishing my first cup when my email chimed. It was Horsmon telling me that he was waiting for Dave Silcock, the Mackay officer. They were going to hit the camp as soon as they could.

The second interruption was a call from Deputy Stratton. I filled him in on what Dowling had told me about sending his boys home. The timing had happened shortly after he had done his knock-and-talk and put Dowling on the fight.

"That's too much of a coincidence," Stratton said. "He's gotta know it was them."

"Absolutely. He was probably doing the same stuff thirty years ago, told me they were stealing beer." I took a sip of coffee and wondered if Dowling had stolen his dad's beer before he went off to prison. "I saw a track in the camp that was from the same shoe as the one in your evidence photo."

"I don't suppose you got a picture, did you?"

"Too busy watching my ass."

When we hung up, my mind went back to the camp, to the girl who had been petting Nick. I had no idea who she was, or who her parents were. I wondered if she'd been the one that had written the word "penis" on the wall.

After three hours, I was just about done with my rough draft when Horsmon called.

"You lied to me, Latham. There weren't four elk in the creek. There were eight."

I was stunned. Why hadn't I worked them one more night? "Jesus Christ. They use my undercover tag?"

"No, the new ones were killed yesterday evening. Guys from Pennsylvania tagged them. You didn't tell me how many shittin' people were gonna be there. Glad I took Silcock."

"Whose tags were on the first four?"

I could hear Horsmon flipping through a notebook. "Gerald Dowling, Claude Dowling, Leroy Barnes, and Jake Smith. Claude's and Jake's were validated for the 3rd. Gerald's and Leroy's were notched for the 2nd.

I did the math. That camp had killed eleven elk. I was sure that five were illegal and I assumed that Barnes had used his ATV to drive the elk out of Big Creek last night, which would make these freshly killed elk illegal too. That brought the number of illegal elk up to nine, but I couldn't see how we were going to prove these last four. I'd dropped the ball.

"Was the guy with the crooked ears there?"

Horsmon snorted. "No, but I cut the shit out of my thumb sawing off the lower jaws for DNA samples. Told them the biologists wanted to age them. There's a gal claimed she's a nurse. Said she'd sew me up. Was flashing her boobs and freaking Silcock out."

"That's Trixie. You get her number?"

Horsmon snorted. "Dowling was sweating blood. He's hinked up. Kept saying everything was legal. Said they were off the road and within a mile. Said it several times."

"Anything else?"

"He told me that Bill Molony and his boys got three elk and took them home."

After we hung up, I saw the case teetering like a seesaw. Every hunter in that camp had now tagged an elk. I could assume the Pennsylvanians would be gone tomorrow. We had nothing on them and they were of little value to the rest of the case. I was sure they'd heard Dowling bragging in camp, but whiskey tales don't make testimony. Those hunters and the elk they had killed were history.

I felt I was close to being able to charge Dowling with four elk; I was fairly sure the lab could determine the tissue samples from at least two of the three kill sites were elk; Horsmon had seen the elk he tagged and validated for Saturday. But the problem with the case was that when it all shook out, Dowling could recant what he'd told me, claim it was a drunken brag and say that somebody else killed the three elk on Friday. If those first three counts flew the coop, it would make his Saturday elk legal and alpha-dog Dowling would be back in the Pahsimeroi killing elk next year. We had to get beyond Dowling's ego and closer to the truth.

We needed to obtain meat samples from the elk that Molony had taken so the lab could forensically compare them with the DNA samples we'd collected from the gut piles. That would take a search warrant, assuming we could figure out where they were. In order for a judge to sign a warrant, I would need to articulate three elements. All three had to be based on facts and speculation wouldn't cut it. The first was that the elk had probably been killed illegally, which of course would be an easy task. The second was that a judge had to conclude–from what I wrote in the affidavit–that the meat would more than likely be at the place we wanted to search. Dowling's story about Molony taking them home wasn't enough for that element. Home could mean Pocatello. The third element was that the information had to be fresh.

Freshness in the legal word is a highly subjective term. If a reliable source says he saw a bighorn sheep head on the subject's wall last month, a judge might conclude that it is reasonable to expect it to still be there. But if the source says he saw thawed steaks from the sheep in the guy's refrigerator a week ago, the judge would deem the information too stale and refuse to issue the warrant.

Somehow, I needed to figure out where those three elk had ended up and then pounce in a reasonable time.

# Chapter 28

I was pulling my hair out, so I called Marc Arms in Pocatello. He had taken a look at Molony's residence and said it was a singlewide sitting in a trailer park surrounded by a sea of similar trailers. He had also done some sleuthing and discovered that Molony's wife was the manager of the park.

"I went ahead and checked the game cutter's logs here in Poky and came up with zippo. Nothing under Molony's name."

I thought about that. Meat cutters charge between $150 and $200 to cut and wrap an elk. "I can't see Molony shelling out $600."

"Probably doing his own butchering." Arms paused. "It'd take two freezers for that much meat. Who the shit has two empty freezers sitting in a house trailer?"

I took a sip of cold coffee and thought about the problem with the warrant. "What's your judge like?"

"It'll probably be Naftz. If we have the PC, he'll issue the warrant. Otherwise we're sucking pond water."

After I hung up, I logged into the Fish and Game's license database and ran the name Molony. I came up with three males in Pocatello—Bill and two juveniles all under the same roof. Sam was fifteen and Brent was sixteen. Both kids had Pahsimeroi antlerless-only elk tags. I knew that Sam had been on the Friday hunt. I remembered Dowling saying that he didn't think Sam had actually killed his elk and Barnes stating he'd recovered a .30-06 bullet from it. The way Barnes had said it made me believe he agreed with his half-brother. So who had killed that elk?

Dowling had talked as if it was just Sam on the hunt, but Claude had used the word "boys" when he'd mentioned Molony's kids. Molony had said he wanted to get his boys an antelope. Was Molony's other kid, Brent, on the Friday killing spree?

Whatever had happened that day, I could picture Dowling and Molony drunk on their butts, showing at least one impressionable kid how to poach. It was disturbing to see a second generation of poachers that some other game warden would have to deal with down the road.

After giving Dowling my cell number, I'd been on edge knowing my phone could buzz at any moment and I'd have to become Pisano by the fourth ring. It was time to grab the cat's tail. I pulled my undercover driver's license out and stared at the photo. I thought about the person I had tried to become; a friendly lawbreaker struggling to kill an elk. I opened up the evidence envelope that held the cigarette pack with his number and caught the smell of tobacco.

Taking a breath, I dialed his number. After a few seconds, a robo-voice asked me if I wanted to leave a message.

"Hey Jerry, Tony Pisano. Just wondering if you guys had any more luck. Give me a call when you get cell service and tell me a hunting story."

\*\*\*\*\*

The following day, I threw a duffel bag together and headed for Pocatello. The route took me along the Salmon River through Ellis. I was leery of running into Dowling, since it wouldn't fit with my IRS lie. I assumed he was still in the Pahsimeroi because he should have had cell service if he was back in Blackfoot.

Something had been nagging me. I found a two-track that snuck down along the river into the cottonwoods. I pulled out the case folder and looked at Barnes' and Dowling's birth dates. The two half-brothers had been born three weeks apart. Claude had been a busy boy when he was twenty-seven, but whatever he was, he'd somehow managed to keep his offspring together.

When I got to the regional office in Pocatello, Arms was there with Eric Crawford, the Regional Investigator from Idaho Falls. Crawford is a slender sandy-hair warden who always seemed to have a grin on his face, despite the fact he's known for his no-bullshit attitude when it comes to violators. Marc Arms is a second-generation warden who is known for investigations that resemble an accountant running a bank audit. Both RI's were wearing civvies with belt badges next to their holstered Glocks.

The two had been trying to scheme some way of determining where the three elk had ended up. The only idea they had come up with was a cold knock-and-talk at Molony's. We agreed that the three elk would probably be tagged by now and that Molony would have a malarkey story created from bits and pieces about the who, what, and where. The challenge for this contact was developing a ruse that explained why two plain-clothes game wardens were

knocking on his door. I told them about the calls from the
two ranchers and we agreed that it would probably be
enough to throw up some camouflage. What I was worried
about was that as soon as they were done, Molony would
call Dowling and manage to connect to his cell. The two
would synchronize their lies and then panic and start
dumping meat.

# Chapter 29

Molony opened his door before Crawford and Arms were on his porch, as if he had been expecting someone. The two RI's rolled their badge wallets and identified themselves.

Arms opened up the conversation. "We got a call from a landowner about some elk that were killed in the Pahsimeroi."

Molony's eyes flared. "I was up there with my two sons teaching them about elk hunting. A friend of mine from Blackfoot's got a trailer up there." He scowled. "This is about that worthless piece of shit rancher. I'm gonna kick his ass if I see him on the road up there."

Arms bit his lip while Crawford responded. "I didn't talk to whoever it was. You guys do any good?"

"I don't hunt up there. Got me a Middle Fork tag, but my boys had cow tags up there. Brought three elk home."

"Three?" Arms asked. "That's a truck load. Who got 'em?"

"My son, Sam, got a little bull calf. Tiny little antlers. Just a calf, so it was all legal."

"Who got the others?" Crawford asked.

"My brother in-law, Roland Milford, got a cow and some guy from Arkansas got another small one."

"Have you got Sam's tag?" Crawford asked.

"Sure, come on in."

Molony found the tag and passed it to Crawford with a shaky hand. It was validated with a kill date of Friday the 31st.

"You bring all the meat off the hill?" Crawford asked.

"Shit yeah, we bring all our meat out. We're not like some pigs. And here's my other kid's tag, clean as a whistle. He didn't get one."

Molony opened the refrigerator door. "Some of it's here and the rest is over at the office. But we brought it all out. We're all legal."

"Anyone else kill elk up there?" Arms asked.

"Christ, there was twenty-two dead elk in that camp. When I seen that slaughter, I said, man this is the way to hunt elk."

"Who's this guy from Arkansas?" Crawford asked.

"I don't know who he is. Had a U-haul. Everybody in that camp's ethical. Everything got tagged. I've never gotten a Fish and Game ticket."

"It all sounds good to me." Arms said.

"Where we camp in the Middle Fork, there's this Anderson game warden. He's a fucker. I told him to get the fuck out of our camp or I'd Claude Dallas his ass and leave him in the backcountry."

Crawford brought the conversation back to the Pahsimeroi. "Twenty-two elk. How many guys were hunting out of that camp?"

"A lot. Everyone up there filled their tags except my boys and a friend of mine, John. He and his boys didn't fill theirs either."

Arms head twisted and he glanced at Crawford. "So your son, Sam, didn't kill an elk?"

Molony's face flushed. "No, I told you, he got this little bull calf."

# Chapter 30

Almost everyone in the office had gone for the night. I could hear two people in the fisheries cubicle talking about pelicans that were eating cutthroat in the Blackfoot River. I was nervously eating a pack of Skittles while waiting for Arms and Crawford to call. My cell buzzed. It was Dowling.

I stepped into the nearest office and put on my Pisano mask. "Jerry, you get me an elk yet?"

"Almost. I got into the fuckers this morning. Getting tired of shittin' in the bushes though. I'm headed home right now. I'll go back next weekend."

I told him a lie about an IRS agent and a second lie when I wished him luck.

Fifteen minutes later, Arms called and we agreed to meet for dinner. We found a restaurant that was nearly empty. They briefed me on the interview while we ate cheap steaks that snuck under the state's $15 dinner limit.

Both officers agreed that Molony was as nervous as a horsefly on a mare's rump. His brag of twenty-two dead elk was a gross exaggeration. I had nailed down eleven elk with this group and was confident with that number. His statement that his sons hadn't killed elk—after stating that his son, Sam, had killed a bull calf—was telling. The three of us had seen this many times. Molony couldn't keep his lies straight. But his back and forth about the elk Sam had tagged meant that something wasn't right about it either.

Milford was a new player. I was sure it would roll out that he had tagged one but hadn't been on the hill when it was killed. Thus he'd picked fruit from the poisonous tree.

The third elk was still a mystery. I was sure that Molony's Arkansas story was woven from whole cloth. He had claimed he didn't know the guy's name from Arkansas and had later spoken the name John. So who really killed it, who tagged it, and where was it? The other nagging thing he'd said was his brag of intimidating a game warden by the name of Anderson. We had two wardens with that last name. Rusty and Steve. Was there any truth to this story? Had he pulled a gun on one of our officers? I added a call to both Andersons to my mental to-do list.

The discussion at dinner boiled down to what we needed to do. I now believed we had enough for search warrants for Molony's residence and the trailer park office. I would write up the affidavit for the warrants after dinner. In the morning, I'd get them printed off at the office and then head to the courthouse for a probable cause hearing. Assuming the judge determined we'd reached the PC bar, we would serve the warrants at 4:00 pm and attempt to interview Dowling, Claude, and Milford to get them on the record with something close to the truth or if they chose, a deep lie. The last missing puzzle piece was to figure out where the third elk went and who tagged it.

# Chapter 31

When I got to my motel room, I booted up my laptop and started cranking on the warrants. With what Arms and Crawford had come up with, I believed the probable cause was golden. But in all my years of working on search warrants, I was never really convinced until I saw it articulated on paper.

A search warrant application is called an affidavit. The process is born from the Constitution's Fourth Amendment: *The right of the people to be secure in their persons, houses, papers, and effects, against unreasonable searches and seizures, shall not be violated, and no warrants shall issue, but upon probable cause, supported by oath or affirmation, and particularly describing the place to be searched, and the persons or things to be seized.*

Arms had managed to covertly take photos of the residence and the office, so the "particularly describing the place to be searched" was fairly straight forward. But there was no room for error. Any defense attorney would get all evidence thrown out if I made even a simple mistake at this point.

Describing the "things to be seized" was easy. We wanted to seize meat and Idaho elk tags that were valid for the Pahsimeroi.

The heart of an affidavit is the probable cause or "PC." The courts have defined this as facts and circumstances within the officer's knowledge that would lead a reasonable person to believe a crime had been committed, and that evidence is located at the place we wanted to search. The courts have also defined what a reasonable person is, but the bottom line with PC is that it's up to a judge to decide if it exists.

My first PC paragraph explained the Pahsimeroi's elk depredation problem and the hunt that that had been developed to deal with it, and that it was limited to within one mile of a cultivated field.

The second paragraph focused on how we had become aware of possible violations and detailed the call Horsmon had gotten from the rancher.

Paragraphs three through eighteen documented the time I spent with Dowling and included many word-for-word quotes, including his story about chasing the wounded cow at seventy and eighty miles an hour along with the tracks in the sage that corroborated his story. The problem I struggled with, was his referencing elk as "fuckers" and "motherfuckers." In all the time I had spent with him, I was sure he had never used the word elk. My challenge was how to articulate my conclusion that he was talking about elk when he used those words. From there, I added the information about the samples from the three gut piles Horsmon and I had collected, the meat seen by Arms and Crawford at Molony's, and the fact that Molony had said he had more meat in the office.

I highlighted the body of the PC with the computer's thumb pad and pasted it into my second affidavit. I completed this document with a description of the trailer park's office. I read the six-page affidavit three times and was convinced a judge would agree we had probable cause. But judges had turned down other officers with this same belief.

Lying down on the motel bed, I closed my eyes and thought about the case. Where the heck was the third elk? Had I missed another Arkansas player? Could Crooked Ears be from Arkansas and had he taken that elk? Or had Barnes taken it back to Arkansas? Molony had mentioned he had a friend named John. Who was he? Who was this Milford guy and what was *his* lie going to be? Would Dowling clam up? Was Molony's Claude Dallas talk a genuine threat, or just his way of throwing out a red herring and puffing up his chest?

# *Chapter 32*

The court clerk opened the judge's chamber door and told me to take a seat. She explained that the judge would be in shortly. I sat on nails in front of his desk and looked around his office. Behind his desk were shelves of legal books that ran to the ceiling. Two black robes hung from a coat rack in the corner. His desktop was organized with a stack of files on one side and a gray multi-line phone on the other. But what caught my eye were the wildlife prints on the walls. Elk, moose and deer set in fields of aspen and sagebrush.

I sat nervously thinking about the justice system. There are laws that bestow rights to people and their families that have been victimized by crime. Because of this, they are notified of court hearings and have the right to be heard at sentencing. When livestock is shot or stolen, unlike wildlife, it's an automatic felony. On the rustling cases I worked, the ranchers aggressively advocated for justice. When prosecutors compose a plea bargains on rustling cases it's done with the rancher's blessing. It's never a sweetheart deal. I think it is because prosecutors are politicians and they know that if they anger one rancher, every rancher in the county will know about it.

Wildlife crimes are handled differently. Most are misdemeanors, and even when the act fits the statutory definition of a felony, prosecutors usually charge or plea them down to misdemeanors. At sentencing, the court room isn't filled with relatives and friends of the victim. The judge looks down on a table with four people. The defendant and his attorney sit on one side, and the prosecutor and the game warden on the other. The court room's pews are empty.

For many years, I brought cases to a judge in Salmon who recognized the value of wildlife. He believed that the great equalizer in justice were jail bars or license revocations. His thinking was that a fine meant one thing to the poor and another to the wealthy, but both understood a week in jail or a year without having hunting privileges. Curiously, when given the choice between jail or a revocation, they all chose jail.

Prosecutors, with few exceptions, were a constant battle. I frequently felt like I was trying to sell them a used car they didn't want to buy when it came to wildlife cases. I had a case where we had purchased a closed-season elk in an undercover investigation. The prosecutor worked out a plea deal where the fine was less than what we'd paid for the elk. In the end, the guy made money from his crime. Fifteen years later it still boils my blood.

I think this disconnect with wildlife crimes stems from the fact that there isn't a property owner or relative to the victim that prosecutors have to face—there's no voting citizen that bumps into his wife at church and asks if he's going to put the man in jail. Several of the prosecutors I worked with seemed to look upon wildlife crimes as if somebody had dumped a pile of trash in the woods. It shouldn't have happened, and it *probably* needed to be prosecuted but there weren't any real victims. They never seemed to grasp the fact that something that had thirsted to live had been killed and stolen from the people of Idaho. To those non-wildlife-supportive prosecutors, illegally taken animals seem to be looked upon as inanimate objects.

Looking at the judge's art prints, I believed Dowling's victims would get a fair shake with these warrants, even though most of the charges would probably be filed in Lemhi and Custer Counties, and heard by other magistrates.

Judge Robert Naftz came in through a side door and introduced himself without offering a handshake. The role of a judge is to take a neutral position and act as a referee to ensure that both sides of a legal issue get a fair shake so this standoffish attitude didn't surprise me but I wondered if he would have taken the same attitude if I'd been an attorney.

Judge Naftz was wearing a long-sleeved white shirt and dress jeans that had been ironed with a crease. He was neatly groomed and tanned, and like most judges his hairline was headed south.

I handed him my affidavits. I explained to him that the probable cause statements in both documents were identical and that I was requesting warrants to search two buildings for the same items.

He slipped on a pair of glasses and began reading. As I watched his eyes, I had second thoughts on whether I should have included Dowling's harsh profanity or whether I should have typed the words with dashed lines that softened his F-bombs.

I watched Naftz face closely when he turned to page four and got into the second paragraph where Dowling had referred to the wounded elk as a motherfucker and bragged about the speed of his chase. The skin on the judge's face blushed like an apple and it was obvious he was upset. I couldn't tell if his anger was directed at me for bringing profanity into his chambers or towards Dowling and his disrespect for wildlife—but wherever it came from, it seemed to bring a chill to the room.

After he had read the last page, the judge turned to a small box to his left. He pushed a button and nodded at me. "We're now on the record in the matter of a request for the issuance of two search warrants. Officer Latham, would you please raise your right hand."

I complied. I studied his face for a ruling but it was like looking at Roosevelt's likeness in the granite of Mount Rushmore. Was there a problem with my affidavit? Had I left some needed legalese from it?

"Officer Latham, do you swear that the statements in these documents are true and accurate?"

"I do."

"I've reviewed the officer's affidavits and find that probable cause exists for issuance of warrants in this matter."

For the moment, the seesaw had my feet on the ground.

# *Chapter 33*

The raid briefing started at 2:00 pm and took place in the basement of the Fish and Game office. There were seven uniform Fish and Game Conservation Officers (game wardens), two Bannock County deputies, a U.S. Fish and Wildlife Special Agent and three RI's. Most of the uniforms were assigned to the search warrants.

District Conservation Officer Steve Anderson would be the supervisor in charge of the warrants. The deputies had been requested in case narcotics were found, which is common with wildlife warrants, and Anderson had also wanted them there in case Molony's Claude Dallas threat was more than a bar-stool brag. I'd checked with officer Rusty Anderson to see if he remembered an incident that fit. He told me he'd never had an issue with a 6'6" hunter. Steve and I believed it was bluster, but the two deputies would initially be in charge of babysitting Molony during the search.

One warden would be assigned to video tape the warrant services. He would do a walk-through with the camera prior to the search and then after they were done, he'd perform the same task so we'd have a before and after video record. This was done because it's common for subjects of a search warrant to trash their own home after the officers leave in an odd attempt to throw water on the case.

Anderson would team up with another officer and the two would perform the actual search. Anything they found that was covered by the warrant would be photographed, tagged, and listed on an inventory. They would only be able to search those areas that one would expect to find meat and game tags.

Crawford and Arms had gone through my report and developed raid packets for the interviews of Dowling, Claude, and Milford. Each packet contained photographs of the subjects, criminal histories, addresses, a list of interview questions and a copy of my twenty-two page report with highlighted sections that were important to that particular interview.

SA Scott Bragonier and RI Eric Crawford were assigned to chase down and interview Claude Dowling and Roland Milford. We'd brought Bragonier into the operation since Claude, although not a tribal member, lived on the Fort Hall Reservation. We needed Bragonier's federal status for jurisdictional issues–plus he's a damn good game warden. A driver's license photo of Milford wasn't available, but Arms had discovered he'd been recently arrested for aggravated battery and managed to get a copy of his booking photo.

I pulled Milford's photo out of his packet in hopes that he'd be my missing Crooked Ears. In the photo, he was standing in front of a height chart, holding a sign with his name and birth date on it. He wore a crooked smile that was odd for someone facing prison for his battery charge, but he wasn't Crooked Ears.

Gerald Dowling's interview was assigned to RI Arms and officer Scott Wright. The two had worked many interrogations together and were superbly talented for this critical task.

Tom Burkhart and I would remain in the office to perform any support and coordination functions that came up. We would also be available to pursue any new leads that developed. The last thing we needed at this phase was for me to be seen by any of the Patterson crew. They'd find that out soon enough.

# Chapter 34

When the officers arrived at the trailer court, both the office and the residence were empty and locked. Entrance was gained with the help of a locksmith. There were three aggressive dogs in the residence. An animal control officer responded and shut them in a bedroom. Several packages of meat, wrapped in butcher paper and labeled, "elk" were located in both buildings and seized. Oddly, Sam Molony's tag was found lying on the ground in the backyard along with an elk skin. Both were seized. As the group was finishing up, Molony's wife Martha arrived with their two sons, Brent and Sam, in a beat-up Buick. She said she had called her husband, told him what was going on, and he was afraid he would be arrested if he came home.

Officer Blake Philips listened to Sam ramble about his elk but he seemed to be making up the story as he went. Martha repeated three times, without being asked, that they only had one elk. Philips believed she was part of a conspiracy to hide the other two elk. It was clear she was upset, but her anger seemed to be pointed to her husband and not at the officers. When Philips asked her about the elk Roland Milford had gotten, she stammered that he had taken an elk heart home with him, but hadn't gotten an elk.

\*\*\*\*\*

Bragonier and Crawford found Claude in an old singlewide trailer sitting beside a hodgepodge of other trailers that looked like aluminum-sided tombstones. Dead rusting vehicles were scattered around the lot like boulders. His wooden porch was sun cracked and gray, and groaned when they stepped on it.

Claude invited them in. His balding wife puttered in the kitchen and acted like she had the place to herself. Claude sat down on a crumpled recliner that fit him like a catcher's mitt. Bragonier and Crawford sat down on a saggy couch that smelled of mold.

"Claude, the reason we're here," Crawford explained, "is that we need to find out who killed the elk you tagged."

Claude looked down at his bare feet. He seemed resigned but didn't answer.

After a bit, Bragonier added. "It's a big deal to me that you didn't waste any meat. I'm hoping you brought it all off the hill."

Claude brought his hands together and interlocked his fingers like he was going to pray. "It's in the freezer on the porch. Some guy from Poky shot it; Ted or Todd. Young kid. He had too many down. Ask me if I wanted it. I did, so I gutted it. Shit, I'm disabled, you know?"

"Who were you with?" Crawford asked.

"Me and my boy Ernie. He's from Pennsylvania. We was driving down the old dry-bed road and ran into this kid. Was in a hell of a hurry. Driving a red Dodge truck... no, it was black. I think it was a Ram Charger, one of them fancy wagons."

"There was a Tony Pisano in your camp a couple of times." Bragonier said. "You told him your son Jerry killed an elk last year that you tagged."

Claude's face blanched, after a moment he shook his head and said, "Huh-uh, don't know who you're talking about. I killed an elk last year. My son Jerry killed one for me the year before. I didn't even fire a shot this year."

Bragonier pulled a topographic map from the raid packet. He passed it to Claude with a pencil and asked, "Show me where that guy killed your elk."

Claude put on a pair of reading glasses and moved his cracked finger across the map. He finally put an X on it that was well outside the one-mile open area.

"Who all brought elk down here from the camp?" Bragonier asked.

"Lemme see... my three sons and me. Then there was Milford, he took one... and Bill's boy Sam and his buddy."

Crawford's head twisted. "Bill Molony's buddy? Who's that?"

"John something or other."

Crawford leaned in. "Where's he live?"

"Pocatello."

"Who killed the elk Milford took home?" Bragonier asked.

Claude's shoulder's slumped and he looked at his toes. "I don't know. It was in the creek for a couple of days. He just came up one day and got it."

Bragonier and Crawford seized Claude's meat and gave him a receipt. His wife never said a word.

# Chapter 35

Arms and Wright drove thirty miles to Blackfoot and called Dowling using the number he'd given me on the Camel wrapper. He picked up on the fifth ring. Arms identified himself and asked if he would come to the Bingham County Sheriff's office. Curiously, Dowling didn't ask what it was about. Twenty minutes later, he walked through the front door of the sheriff's office looking like a dog was going to jump out and bite him.

He had on faded jeans with one blown-out knee, a dirty white T-shirt and his skin was as tan as a sailor. His stained yellow ball cap was perched on his head.

Arms and Wright took him back to an interview room that was about the size of a bathroom. The walls were painted white and had a wainscot of gray speckled carpet. The room was crammed with a desk and three chairs. Dowling took a seat in the back corner. Arms took the next seat and Wright took the seat in front of the door.

Arms read Dowling his Miranda rights and asked if he understood them.

"I do, but I don't get why I'm here."

Arms nodded his head. "It involves some elk in the Pahsimeroi."

"I tagged mine and I was already checked."

"When did you kill your elk?"

"On the 2nd. My tag's in the my freezer with my meat."

"How many elk were killed on the 2nd?"

"Just mine and my brother's." Dowling dropped his head and brought his left hand to his forehead like he had a headache. His other hand covered his crotch. "Sam got one, I think Roland Milford. I'm not sure. My brother was here from Pennsylvania, my other brother was here from Arkansas. There was so many people I can't tell you the dates when those fuckers was killed."

Arms set his raid packet on the desk. "Before we go any farther, I need to be upfront with you. We know what happened up there. Everything. It's going to be imperative that you're honest with us."

Dowling leaned towards Arms. "I'll tell you whatever went down up there. I know I was legal."

Arms looked him in the eye. "You killed more elk than the one on the $2^{nd}$."

Dowling shook his head like he had water in his ears.

Arms dug in. "Is that sounding a little familiar?"

Dowling's chin started to get slick with sweat. "No, I haven't killed more elk than that."

"How about on the $31^{st}$?"

"The $31^{st}$?"

Arms nodded. "Let's just back up, 'cause you're wondering how we know what we know. You know a guy named Tony up there. Tony Pisano that was in your camp."

Dowling sat back like he was trying to get away. He crossed his arms and brought his feet up on the chair's base in a near fetal position. "He was hunting but... I never had any elk on the $31^{st}$. He left me his tag and I wasn't gonna shoot his elk. It's still in my jockey box."

Arms nodded. "I'll tell you what. Tony is one of our officers. He works for us. And he was with you in that camp and he knows about the elk that you killed on the 31st."

Dowling seemed frozen but after a bit he covered his mouth with his fist. "I didn't shoot any of them. I can tell you who shot them."

Arms shook his head. "You're going down the wrong path. But if you want to continue, that's your choice."

Wright jumped in. "Let me tell you the little bit I know, Jerry."

Dowling was leaning as far away as he could get in the tiny room. His arms were clamped tight to his chest. His hands were buried in his armpits. His head was slowly rocking back and forth.

"Tony's down here. I've worked with him quite a bit."

Dowling's head began nodding like a bobblehead doll.

"We've found the three gut piles from the 31st." Wright explained. "We have brass from your rifle, your three-hundred mag. Kinda like Marc was telling you, we're not asking you if you did it. We're telling you we already know what happened. The biggest thing we'd like to confirm is that the elk that were shot, they all have tags on them."

Dowling relaxed and nodded. "Yes, they're tagged."

Arms scooted his chair closer. "Where are the elk that were killed that day?"

"Sam's, Milford's... I can't remember... I think there was only two that were shot that day."

Arms picked up his raid packet and looked at a page. "There were three elk killed on the 31st."

Dowling's head continued its bobblehead dance.

"There's three gut piles and brass from your rifle." Wright said.

Dowling sat frozen, but his head continued the short side-to side swing. "There's two-forty-three brass and thirty-thirty and thirty-ought-six brass up there too. Because Milford shoots thirty-thirty and Sam shoots two-forty-three and Molony shoots thirty-ought-six."

Arms thumbed through his packet. "Have you talked to Molony recently?"

Dowling shook his head.

"We talked to him last night and he said there were three elk killed on the 31st. We know there were three elk killed on the 31st."

Dowling shook his head. "I didn't hit a one of them."

Wright brought him back to reality. "You told Tony you chased that elk at eighty miles an hour after shooting from a thousand yards and hit it in the ass and then when it went down, you said you shot it again in the head."

Arms added, "And you told him you shot the two up on the hill and you said you hit the one out on the flat in the ass."

Dowling nodded. "I hit the one in the ass."

"When this comes into court," Wright said, "it's not gonna look good when you're not being honest. It's gonna look really bad for you."

"I'm being as honest as I can, but I didn't shoot three fucking elk." Dowling's bobblehead returned. "I shot one elk."

Arms leaned back. "You're claiming you shot one elk on the 2nd, which we are aware of. And Leroy Barnes killed an elk on the 2nd, and there were three elk killed by you on the 31st."

Dowling nodded. "There was two killed on the hill."

Arms nodded. "Three elk killed by you on the 31st. Two on the hill and the one in the flat."

"I did not kill three fucking elk."

"You told Tony you killed the two up on the hill and the one in the flat." Wright said.

Arms shook his head. "We talked to Molony. They didn't kill those elk. Sam tagged one."

Dowling leaned in and tapped his finger on the desk. "Yes he did. Sam was right there. He killed that elk."

Arms brought his palm up. "You tell us your version then."

"We was in my truck. We went up there and we started shooting."

Arms brought his hand up and pointed at Dowling. "On the 31st, when those three elk were killed, who was with you?"

Dowling open his right hand and started flicking his fingers out. "Molony, his two sons, Sam and Brent."

Arms asked, "So who killed the three elk on the 31st?"

"Sam killed a little bull. Its horns were about as big as my fingers."

"I know he has one of them," Arms shook his head. "What else was killed on the 31st?"

Dowling continued using his fingers to count. "There was another cow that was mine. There was another... I think it was a calf. They were all firing at those fuckers. I wasn't the only one shooting. It was late in the afternoon.

Molony and I had been drinking all afternoon. I'll tell you right now. He killed one of them. I wasn't the only one shooting."

Wright shook his head. "Let's back up, cause I'm kind of a simpleton. On the 31st, there were three elk killed. Two up on the hill and the one you hit in the ass and chased down."

"Right, I hit her in the ass so I had to go get her."

"So who was there that afternoon?"

"Molony and..."

"And he's shooting."

"Yeah, he's shooting."

"And he doesn't have a tag." Wright pointed out.

Dowling's head nodded. "And he didn't have a tag."

"What kind of rifle was he shooting?"

"Thirty-ought-six. And Sam was there, two-forty-three and Brent, his other boy was shooting a thirty-thirty."

"The four of you shooting. Who tagged them?"

"I tagged one, Sam tagged one, and I believe Brent tagged the other one, I'm not sure."

Arms brought his palms up. "Brent's tag is unvalidated. He didn't tag an elk."

"Roland Milford tagged the elk. That's where it went."

Wright cut in. "Was Roland even there?"

"No."

"So he put his tag on an elk..." Wright trailed off.

Dowling nodded. "That Molony gave him."

"That Molony killed."

Dowling leaned back to the wall. "I don't know who killed it. All of us was shooting. I didn't hit one for sure until I hit the one in the ass that I tagged."

144

"On the 31ˢᵗ," Arms said. "On that day, you killed one."

Dowling nodded, "Uh-huh."

Wright asked, "And is that the day on your tag, the 31ˢᵗ?"

Dowling smiled and clenched his fists back into his armpits. "I don't know the date. It's in the deepfreeze at home."

"Where's your brother Leroy Barnes?" Wright asked.

"He's back in Arkansas."

Arms looked at his notes. "That's where Leroy lives, isn't it?"

"Part of the time."

"Which part of the time are you talking about?" Arms asked.

Dowling leaned back and locked his fingers together over his belt buckle. "He delivers boats for a bass boat company back there."

"Full time?" Arms asked.

"He does."

Arms pulled a map out of his packet and set it on the desk. "Are you familiar with the one-mile rule up there?"

"I am."

Arms pulled an aerial photo out with the locations of the three gut piles. Each kill site had a one-mile radius drawn in red around it that showed they were all over a mile from the distance to a field.

"I didn't kill all those elk. I was there, but I didn't shoot all of them. I told you, everybody was shooting. Molony took all three elk."

Arms shook his head. "What you're telling us and what Molony said are two different stories. I don't know who's trying to cover whose ass, but it isn't working."

Wright kicked in, "Molony took all three of those elk. Your saying Sam killed one, you killed one, and Molony killed one."

Dowling leaned back, crossed his legs and put his hands back in his armpits. "I don't know if Molony killed one, but he was shooting."

Wright pressed him. "How did Molony give that elk to Milford if he didn't kill it?"

"He took it, but I can't say for sure if he killed it. Sam tagged one, I tagged the one I hit and Milford tagged the other one."

At this point, Dowling had claimed he had killed an elk on the 2nd, used his tag on it and that he *hadn't* killed one on the 31st. He then changed his story: He had said he killed one on the 31st and had used his tag on it. He didn't understand that the two wardens were good listeners.

# *Chapter 36*

Wright played the science card. "Jerry, the DNA from the gut pile out there on that flat is going to match the DNA from the elk you tagged and you say is in your freezer. Is that what you're telling me?"

"No, just like I said. I killed my elk the other day on the 2nd. Molony took all three of those fuckin' elk."

Wright leaned in to close the deal. "What about the elk you shot in the ass?"

"I shot it in the ass and Molony took that elk... you want the truth? I'll give you the fuckin' truth." Dowling's shoulders slumped; he leaned towards Arms and opened both palms. "I shot that fucking elk on the 31st in the ass and Molony took it. I shot the elk in my freezer on the 2nd and tagged it... you need to understand we was drunk that night and I chased the one I hit in the ass. Then I shot it in the head. We loaded all three in my truck and took them back to camp. Molony left with all three. I don't know who tagged the other two. We was both shit-faced."

Arms pressed him. "How'd Milford end up tagging the elk you killed on the 31st?"

"Molony told him to tag it."

"And you were okay with him tagging that elk, an elk you had killed?"

Dowling nodded. "It needed a tag."

Arms clicked his pen. "On the 2nd, you and Leroy went out and each killed an elk."

"Yeah, we wasn't on the road. There was a field right there. We tagged them. We was all legal."

"Let me make sure I have this straight," Wright said. "You and Molony and his two boys killed three elk on the 31st. All three of those elk were outside the one-mile open area. You hauled all three elk in your truck back to camp. And then you killed another elk on the 2nd, is that right?"

Dowling looked at his hands like he'd lost something. "It is."

"Your dad's elk. Tell me how he ended up with it," Wright asked.

"He didn't kill it. Some kid came down the dry wash and said he had killed two. No idea who the kid is. I wasn't there."

"You have any problem taking us to your home and showing us that tag?" Wright asked.

"No problem."

Arms studied his notes. "What's your relationship with Milford?"

"He's my ex-brother in-law. Just moved back from Alaska."

Arms opened my report. "This is what you told Tony. *That's where I shot that last cow up. Those are my tracks. I chased that motherfucker at seventy and eighty miles an hour. I came off this hill and shot straight across that fucking flat.'*

Dowling nodded. "That's the one."

Arms pulled out the aerial photo showing the gut pile locations, the one-mile radius, and the distance to the green fields. "These two elk that died next to each other–that tells me they dropped right where they were shot. Is that right?"

Dowling nodded. "Yeah, they were all bunched up and the two they hit fell like bricks."

Arms looked up and the room was quiet for maybe a minute. "Sam tagged one," Arms said, "Milford tagged one, but who tagged the other one?"

"I don't know. Molony had some friend there by the name of John or Johnny from Pocatello. Had some homemade trailer. He and his two kids was sleeping in it. They slipped that calf in there. All three of them had tags." Dowling's arms were wide apart with his palms facing Wright. "I'm telling you the truth. I'm telling you everything I know."

Wright nodded. "I think we're getting pretty much the straight story from you. But when you're interviewing someone, if they tell you something that turns out it's not the truth, it looks really bad. Judges don't like that."

"I'll take a polygraph test. I didn't shoot the first two."

# *Chapter 37*

The interrogation had lasted an hour and a half. Both wardens believed they had finally gotten Dowling to tell the truth about the three elk, but two elk were still in the wind.

Arms and Wright had followed Dowling to his home. They seized the meat. His tag was validated for the 2nd. They also seized my undercover tag from his truck. While they were loading the meat, Dowling mentioned that Barnes was probably still hanging out at his girlfriend's house and his meat was more than likely at the local butcher shop.

They drove to the butcher's and found Barnes' elk in four big coolers, gave the butcher a receipt and loaded the meat in their truck.

Arms had printed a list of everyone with Pahsimeroi elk tags and had stuck it in his raid packet. It's a three and a half hour drive to Patterson, so few people from Pocatello hunt there. With Wright driving, he went through the eighty names and checked off the hunters with local addresses. There were three named John. Arms, being the investigator that he is, found two other tag holders with the same address—it fit what Dowling had told them and they throttled to John Jesson's address.

Jesson was as skinny as a pencil, wore a two-week beard and black hair that looked like it had been pulled out of a Brillo box.

"I knew you were coming. Bill Molony called me an hour ago and told me to come up with a story about the calf."

"How about we cut through the malarkey and save us all some time?" Arms said. "Whose tag did you use on the calf?"

"We used my son's. It had been in the creek a couple of days and people were cutting meat off it. The way they was talking in camp was that Jerry had killed all three, and this was one of 'em. Nobody wanted it since it was so small, so we took it."

Arms and Wright seized what was left of the elk.

I'd been sitting in the office twiddling my thumbs with Tom Burkhart. Crawford had called in and briefed us on the Claude Dowling interview, but Crawford and Bragonier hadn't been able to find Roland Milford. The address he'd claimed during his arrest turned out to be an empty building.

Burkhart got on the department's license database and looked up Milford. It showed an address east of Blackfoot. He knew the area since it was his patrol area. We jumped in his marked truck and headed out.

The address was out in the farmland. We found a singlewide trailer surrounded by hard-packed dirt under a cottonwood that must have been a hundred years old. The place was lit by a yard light. A rusty Chrysler Lebaron was parked out front. A dumpy female answered the door and I showed her my badge wallet.

"Is Roland here?" I asked.

"What's he done now?"

Her response made me wonder if she was the victim of his recent arrest. "Maybe nothing. Is he here?"

She shook her head and glanced back in the trailer. "No. Don't know when he'll show up."

"Where's he live?"

"Wherever. Sometimes his truck."

"Do you have his number?"

"Doesn't have one."

It was clear she didn't want to help. I handed her my business card. "I'm gonna knock on your door twice a day until I find him. You see him, have him call and we can get this worked out."

We got about a mile down the road when my phone rang and showed an unknown number. It was Roland Milford.

"Thanks for calling, you tagged an elk that Bill Molony said you could have. We need to talk."

"How come?"

"Cause my boss is on my ass, so help me out here. Tell me how you got mixed up in this."

"We was in Patterson and my friend Bill brought in three elk. He said I could have one, so I brought it home."

"Who killed it?" I asked.

"Don't know, wasn't around when they killed it."

"Where is it at now?"

"Up on Wolverine. I got a trailer up there."

Burkhart and I drove to Milford's trailer to seize the meat. The odd thing was that he'd told me the door would be unlocked and to just walk in and grab it from the freezer. This was way out of the box, so when I got to the front door, I knocked and after no response, called him back. I turned my recorder on and chatted with him while we bagged up the frozen meat. It had been cut and stuffed in Ziploc bags.

There was only about a third of an elk, but it didn't bother me. We had our three missing elk and I was confident that samples from them would match the DNA from the gut piles.

Each team returned to the office. Boxes filled with hundreds of pounds of frozen meat were separated into heavy black trash bags, tagged and logged into waiting freezers. We met in the basement and debriefed. Each team detailed what they'd seized and what their subjects had said.

The big hinge had been the work done by Arms and Wright. They'd sliced through Dowling's bullshit and gotten to the truth. I didn't need to know whose bullets killed the first two elk since Dowling's admission that he had transported them would work for two counts of unlawful possession. His confession about killing the one that he'd chased and killed illegally on the 31st–the one he claimed he had *'hit in the ass'*–made the elk he killed on the 2nd an over-limit.

By 11:00 PM, we were done and I was beyond tired. It had been a long day. I drove through the darkened streets of Pocatello looking for a quick place to get a burger and fries but everything was closed. I bought two corndogs at a gas station and took them back to my motel room.

I stuck a thumb drive in my computer and started watching the video of Dowling cornered in a box by Arms and Wright. About ten minutes into the interrogation, I fell asleep listening to his voice trying to convince the wardens he wasn't a poacher. I had good dreams that night.

# *Epilogue*

Merritt Horsmon and I interviewed Bill Molony in Challis. He brought his two sons with him and lied for hours. I still find it incredulous that he did this in front of his boys that knew he was lying. He started his whopper out with, "I'll be honest with you." His version of the third elk deviated five miles from Dowling's. For some bizarre reason, he was still trying to protect Jesson. He claimed that two mean-looking men drove up and stole it from them. Towards the end of his lies he said, "and that's no shit." At one point Horsmon thought the 6' 6" man was going to cry. I don't think he ever figured out that I had been the undercover and that we had met in the doorway of his RV.

Dr. Karen Rudolph analyzed twenty-four tissue samples for DNA comparison at the Idaho Fish and Game forensic laboratory. These came from the three kill sites Horsmon and I had located, the eight elk that he and Silcock had checked in the creek, and the meat seized during the raid.

As we thought, the elk that we seized at Molony's matched one of the kill sites on the hill. Jesson's meat matched the other kill site. But you'll recall, the first kill site that Horsmon and I documented had been heavily fed on by scavengers and all that was left was a blood stain in the dirt.

Rudolph was unable to extract DNA from this sample because what little had been present had been degraded by the sun and bacteria for days. The lack of a DNA match from this kill site didn't dampen the case against Dowling. We had his story that he had told me about killing the elk and it was reinforced by his confession that he had told to Wright and Arms.

In order to obtain a certified copy of Leroy Barnes' tax address for court, I had to obtain a search warrant for the Lemhi County Court House. In describing the building, I incorporated the description of the statue of Lady Justice on top of the building, *"The figure is blindfolded. In her left hand she holds a scale with balanced pans. Her right hand holds a sword."*

Lady Justice personifies what our judicial system should be. Her blindfold represents impartiality and the ideal that justice ignores power and wealth. The scales represent her weighing the facts of both sides of a case without prejudice. The sword represents her authority and that her justice can be swift and final.

*****

## Dowling's Boys

Lemhi County was unable to link Dowling's sons to the Patterson School vandalism and the case closed when the statue of limitations ran its course.

In 2015 one of the Dowling boys had an arrest warrant issued in Blackfoot after he failed to appear in court. The county received a tip that he might be hiding out in

Patterson. Their source said he had bragged he'd go down shooting. Sheriff's deputies suited up and found him drinking coffee at the campfire in from of the Patterson cabin. They arrested him without incident.

## Roland Milford

Milford told me that he had moved back to Idaho in April. His license history showed that a month later he purchased a resident fishing license. In Idaho, and most other states, a person must reside for six months before attaining resident privileges.

On October 2, 2007, a month after the raid, I charged him with the *unlawful possession* of the elk and the *fraudulent purchase* of a resident license, both committed in Lemhi County.

On March 18, 2008, he pleaded guilty to both counts. Judge Stephen Clark fined him $683 and revoked his hunting privileges for two years. Two years later, he hadn't paid his fine and Judge Clark issued a warrant for his arrest.

On a dark October night in 2015, Milford pulled into an all-night Fish and Game check station north of Salmon. When game warden Chad Wippermann shined his flashlight into the vehicle, Milford was drinking a beer. Whipperman asked him to dump it out. Milford chose to drink it. Wippermann ran his driver's license, discovered the warrant and hooked him. He spent the night in the Lemhi County jail and the following day he was put on formal probation. As I write this ten years after he tagged the elk, he still owes the court $283.

## John Jesson

I charged Jesson on October 5, 2007, with the *unlawful possession* of an elk in Bannock County. This was predicated on the fact that he tagged an elk that had been killed unlawfully. This was the same legal basis for Milford's charge. The court appointed a public defender who managed to talk prosecutor Lance Stevenson into dismissing the charge. Perhaps Stevenson had a good reason for dumping it, but it wasn't for lack of evidence.

## Claude Dowling

On December 13, 2007, Claude was charged with *unlawful possession* of an elk for the same reasons Milford and Jesson got their citations. He was fined $583 and lost his hunting privileges for two years.

His admission that he had tagged an elk–that Dowling had killed two years prior to this elk–came too late. There's a two-year statute of limitations on most Fish and Game violations and the deadline had run its course a week prior to the raid.

## Ernie Dowling

You'll recall that he was there when Claude took possession of an illegal elk killed by an unknown subject. Since Ernie transported it in his truck, I charged him with the *unlawful possession* of the elk on January 18, 2008. He called the court from Pennsylvania and entered a guilty plea. The judge fined him $418, and he sent a check to the court.


## Bill Molony

I charged Molony with three counts of *principle to the unlawful possession* of elk and one count of *hunting without a valid tag*—all in Custer County. He retained an attorney who worked out a plea agreement that dismissed two counts and allowed him to enter a guilty plea to one.

Judge Charles Roos fined him $333 and revoked his hunting privileges for three years. He also ordered that for each of those three years, he speak to a Hunter Education Class and tell the students about his violations. He was also mandated he read Jim Posewitz's, *Beyond Fair Chase* and write a three-page essay about the book. Barnes never did write his report and I suspect he has yet to read the book.


## Sam and Brent Molony

Fifteen-year old Sam and his sixteen-year old brother were victims of their upbringing. They were hunting—and I use that term lightly since chasing elk with pickups isn't what real hunters call hunting—with two drunken adults. I'm not surprised they did what they did. Three years prior to that bloody day, the two attended a Hunter Education Course in order to qualify for hunting licenses. The class appears to be written for the Molonys; it involves twelve to eighteen hours of safety, ethics, and game laws.

There's a point where a person needs to be responsible for his own behavior, so I charged Sam for *unlawful possession* of the spike bull and Brent for *attempting to take elk in a closed area*. Their father's attorney managed to get both charges dismissed if they re-attended a Hunters Education Course.

### Leroy Barnes

Barnes' residency case was as clear as crystal. He had told me he lived in Arkansas. His brother had said the same to Arms and Wright. He was having his property-tax bill sent to Arkansas, and his truck was also registered there.

He had been running this scam for seven years, and only two of those years were still within the two-year statute of limitations. I was able to charge him with five counts of *unlawful licenses and tag purchases* that he had committed in those two years.

Those counts were in Bingham County. Prosecutor J. Scott Andrews in a plea agreement, dropped two counts and Barnes entered a guilty plea to three. Judge Scott Hansen assessed fines of $990 and revoked his hunting privileges for three years. He was also assessed a civil forfeiture of $1254 for the money he had defrauded Idaho in those two years.

Barnes killed his elk just inside Lemhi County (using his illegal tag and license). Prosecutor Paul Withers, in a plea agreement, changed the charge to the unlawful purchase of a resident elk tag and Judge Stephen Clark fined him $100.

In 2010, Officer Andy Smith cited him for purchasing a hunting license and elk tag while revoked. Prosecutor J. Scott Andrews, in a plea agreement, dismissed one count and Barnes entered a guilty plea to the remaining charge. Judge Ryan Boyer fined him $100.

### Gerald Dowling

I charged Dowling with six counts; *take elk unlawful* (for the first elk he chased down with his pickup), two counts of *principle to the unlawful possession of elk* (for the two elk killed on the hill), *hunt elk with the aid of a motorized vehicle*, and two counts of *attempt to take elk over limit* for the days he hunted with me. All these charges were filed in Custer County and each held a possible sentence of six months in jail. I wanted to charge him with the elk he tagged in Lemhi County since it was a clear over-limit but prosecutor Paul Withers believed the charges in Custer were enough and declined prosecution.

Dowling retained an attorney and the litigation dance began. His lawyer filed a notice that they would be using an alibi defense. I'm still scratching my head on how they thought that scheme might work. Perhaps they thought Pisano would cover for them.

From the get-go, I knew this case wouldn't go to trial— we had him cold. A Challis jury would recoil against his disrespect for elk.

Finally, after six months of motions and hearings that must have cost him thousands, Dowling plead to three counts for the three elk he and the Molonys had killed on their high-speed adventure.

Judge Charles Roos assessed fines, court costs and civil penalties of $2,025. He revoked his hunting privileges for nine years, and put him in jail for ten days. Keep in mind that Judge Roos has a deep respect for the land and wildlife. He was one of the finest judges I brought cases to. Many judges would have allowed Dowling's revocation to run concurrently, three years instead of nine.

Dowling signed a payment plan with the court and failed to meet payment deadlines fourteen times but after repeated threats of arrest, he finally paid up.

In September 2010, game warden Andy Smith got a tip that there was a dead bull elk stashed in Patterson Creek. The green-field hunt had been eliminated and the only elk season open in the Pahsimeroi was for archery.

Smith slipped through the cottonwoods and found a five-point bull and two freshly killed cow elk in the creek. They were tied up just like Dowling had done in 2007. All three were tagged by men from Pennsylvania. The two cows were tagged with antlerless-only permits that were valid in the Lemhi Valley, which is an hour and half drive from

Patterson. The bull had several bullet wounds and was tagged with an archery permit.

Smith snuck out and called warden Malcolm Clemenhagen for backup. The two drove into the camp and found seven intoxicated hunters. When Smith stepped out of his truck, Jerry Dowling yelled out, "Fuck ya, you pricks ain't gettin' me again," and raced for his truck. Smith believed he was going for a gun. In a commanding shout he ordered him to stop... and he complied.

The person who had tagged the bull claimed he'd shot it legally with his bow—which Smith asked him to produce but after some hemming and hawing, he admitted he'd left it in Pennsylvania. After Smith pointed out the bullet wounds, the guy confessed to shooting it with a rifle.

Smith and Clemenhagen arrested the shooter and hauled him to jail. The two drunks who had tagged the cows claimed they'd shot them in the Lemhi Valley but couldn't describe how they drove there. For several days, the two wardens drove the Pahsimeroi looking for magpies and ravens working gut piles but weren't able to find them.

*****

There were four phases to this case; the rancher who made the call, my undercover work, the overt investigative effort by Horsmon, Arms, Crawford, Wright and several other officers. And finally the litigation and sentencing phase conducted by the prosecutors and judges after we had filed the twenty-three charges.

The reader might conclude that our judicial system dropped the ball—that Lady Justice's sword has become slow and dull—it's something I lived with throughout my career. Society, as a whole, is disgusted with wildlife crime. But most judges and prosecutors aren't drinking from the same bucket. Few that I worked with, had a deep appreciation for wildlife and they didn't take these crimes seriously. It's partly because their workload is over shadowed by crimes like rape and other violent acts committed against people. But that's a simplification of the problem. There's more to it.

In the early years of Idaho, the legislature created one magistrate and one prosecutor for each county. As the population grew, cities, counties and state agencies added officers to deal with the increased crime but failed to shore-up the other leg of the system—additional prosecutors and magistrates. The courts have responded to this untenable workload with what is called *judicial economy*. Their answer is a justice system that relies on skinny plea bargains that often resemble a hungry dog chewing on sun-bleached bones.

To understand the positive side of the Patterson case, one needs to step back and look down at the Pahsimeroi from the Donkey Hills. Do this while the valley floor is still pooled with quiet darkness and the sun is climbing up the backside of the Lemhis. Do it while the Shoshone's ancient gem is whisper quiet. As you look from that sagebrush point, think about the effect this case had on Jerry Dowling and the people who live in the Pahsimeroi.

The Pahsimeroi residents recognize that we did our job. We caught Dowling and seven of his miscreant friends. Those people who live in the valley know that when they call Idaho Fish and Game, a Conservation Officer will respond and do his or her job.

One has to recognize that Dowling is a recidivist. There's no punishment that will change him. He will always be an outlaw. Prison didn't stop his drinking and driving. I'd be willing to bet that while I was scratching out this story, he drove drunk and during his nearly decade long hunting-license revocation, he hunted and killed.

But look closer. Slide onto the dusty seat of Dowling's truck. Inhale his sweat and watch his eyes flick about. Dowling fears game wardens even more now than when I ran with him. I'm sure when he's out in the hills and runs into a stranger, he's suspicious. When he sees a dust trail kicking up from an unknown vehicle, he gets nervous. It can't be fun. In the hills, he's haunted and I'd like to believe that from time to time, Tony Pisano walks into his dreams.

# Also by Tony H. Latham

Non-fiction:

*Analyzing Ballistic Evidence, On-Scene by the Investigator*

*Trafficking, A Memoir of an Undercover Game Warden*

And for the reader that craves a mystery/thriller on a dark winter night, you might fall into the tales of game warden Charley Cove:

*Five Fingers*

*Seven Dead Fish*